The Facial Analysis Diet

Elizabeth Gibaud was born in Scotland.
Having discovered naturopathy at an
early age she went to Africa to study
under the famous naturopath
F. O. Lawrence, before going to
America for two years to research.

She now lives in London where
she practises at the prestigious Hale
Clinic.

The Facial Analysis Diet

Elizabeth Gibaud

Century · London

Published by Century in 2003

1 3 5 7 9 10 8 6 4 2

Copyright © Elizabeth Gibaud 2003

Elizabeth Gibaud has asserted her right under the Copyright,
Designs and Patents Act, 1988 to be identified as the author
of this work

First published in the United Kingdom in 2003 by Century

The Random House Group Limited
20 Vauxhall Bridge Road, London SW1V 2SA

Random House Australia (Pty) Limited
20 Alfred Street, Milsons Point, Sydney,
New South Wales 2061, Australia

Random House New Zealand Limited
18 Poland Road, Glenfield, Auckland 10, New Zealand

Random House South Africa (Pty) Limited
Endulini, 5a Jubilee Road, Parktown 2193, South Africa

The Random House Group Limited Reg. No. 954009

www.randomhouse.co.uk

A CIP catalogue record for this book is available
from the British Library

Papers used by Random House are natural, recyclable products made
from wood grown in sustainable forests. The manufacturing processes
conform to the environmental regulations of the country of origin

ISBN 0 7126 23132

Typeset by SX Composing DTP, Rayleigh, Essex

Printed and bound in Great Britain by
Bookmarque Ltd, Croydon, Surrey

I dedicate this book to the greatest naturopath of the twentieth century, Dr F. O. Lawrence.

Note from the publisher

Any information given in this book is not intended to be taken as a replacement for medical advice. Any reader – especially one with a pre-existing medical condition – should consult a doctor first before starting any weight-loss programme. Any person with a condition requiring medical attention should consult a qualified medical practitioner or suitable therapist.

The identities of people described in the case histories have been changed to protect patient confidentiality.

The publisher and author are not responsible for any goods and/or services offered or referred to in this book and expressly disclaim all liability in connection with the fulfilment of orders for any such goods and/or services and for any damage, loss or expense to the person or property arising out of or relating to them.

The publishers have made all efforts to check that the food products recommended in this book are available in this country, and concede that some may only be found in specialist health food shops or grocers.

Acknowledgements

Grateful thanks for the invaluable contribution to the book are extended to my editor, Hannah Black, and my agent Kay McCauley.

Contents

Introduction

I was just three years old when I first trod the boards of the theatre; at seven I joined the Joyce Delany dance troupe at the local church hall in Shoreditch; at ten I graduated to Miss Terry's Juvenile Theatre School in the heart of London's West End. Determined to impress Miss Terry, I worked hard and was soon singing and dancing with comedians such as Arthur Askey, Tommy Trindler and Charlie Chester. Then, after winning a scholarship to the Royal Ballet School, I spent the next five years dancing and singing at Sadlers Wells.

It was during this time, whilst somersaulting over ten barrels, that I damaged a disc in my spine and so changed my life and direction for ever.

In 1960, when I was in my late teens, I awoke one morning unable to move my lower limbs. My legs felt as though they had been dislocated from my torso. The pain was excruciating. The prognosis was grim. The family doctor examined me and advised an immediate operation to remove the damaged disc and fuse the discs either side together. He warned me that this was the only way in which I could hope to avoid becoming wheelchair-bound before I turned thirty. The future was bleak.

Left with the doctor's grim diagnosis echoing in my ears there was much to consider and my mind flashed back to when I was a small child living in our family home in London, where Grandpops had occupied the attic. Grandpops suffered from emphysema and had coughed and spluttered all through my childhood. He had been a devout patient, swallowing handfuls of pills and adhering strictly to his doctor's orders, until he was carried out feet first at the age of seventy.

Then there was beautiful Vonne, my elder sister, who had followed the family trait by being confined to her bed every winter suffering from bronchitis and pneumonia. Vonne was subjected to numerous x-rays and swallowed her medication without question until she died, aged just thirty-eight, from breast cancer.

My much-loved Scottish grandma – a diabetic – died after lapsing into a coma, caused by an overdose of insulin accidentally administered by her doctor. And then I thought of her daughter, a conscientious blood donor all her young life until, ironically, she died of leukaemia aged forty-two.

It seemed to me quite evident that the conventional system of health care did not work for my family, so I was wary of submitting to orthodox surgery on my spine. When I succumbed to my annual bout of wheezing and coughing during the damp English winter, I decided to boycott conventional medicine and search for alternative means. I began to hide the pills my mother gave me under my tongue until I could flush them away, and the family doctor finally gave up after chasing me around the bedroom aiming a gigantic syringe at my posterior and inadvertently injecting himself.

I started by collecting alternative dietetic information. I studied books on anatomy, digestion and absorption. I was inspired by the writings of the American dietician Leylord Kordell and the supplement giant Gaylord Hausler. I was enthralled by the British naturopath Harry Benjamin, fascinated by the fruitarian, Professor Ehret, and the famous Lindlair brothers. I followed the instructions of these great pioneers in alternative medicine, studying and reading all the books and literature I could get my hands on. I practised their philosophies. (I became a fruitarian for two years – not something that I would recommend in retrospect, since the high sugar content of fruit is not good for one's health!) In time, I began to experience the greatest feeling of well-being imaginable.

My health was restored and I found I did not suffer with colds, flu or asthma again. With all of this in mind, I became even more determined to avoid surgery on my damaged back and so I continued in my search for a permanent cure the *natural* way. Yoga provided me with the answer; I was able to strengthen my back muscles by practising an exercise called the 'cat hump' (go down on all fours and breathe in and out, alternately arching your back like an angry cat and releasing your back downwards). Repeating this exercise twenty times a day completely restored my back's strength and flexibility and, thankfully, despite the doctor's pessimistic prognosis, no operation was necessary.

However, this was not the end of my interest in alternative health, and it was not long before another event occurred that propelled me to learn much more about the problems that can arise from an imbalanced diet.

In 1969, during a cruise, I met my future husband. We were married the following year in South Africa, where we settled to begin a new life farming dairy and organic vegetables. My blue-eyed, blonde-haired daughter, Catherine, was born in 1971, followed by the birth of my raven-haired,

brown-eyed daughter, Alexandra, in 1976.
However, Alexandra was born with breathing
problems and I was not allowed to see her for the
first twenty four hours. I later discovered that
Alexandra's breathing was laboured and that she
did not respond to the suction procedure
administered directly after birth. Within a few days
I was told Alexandra was well and that we could
take her home.

During the first night home, Alexandra's
breathing was erratic. I slept next to her cot
because on several occasions she appeared to stop
breathing. Knowing what I do now, I realize that
Alexandra's pinhead-sized sinuses were blocked as
a *direct* result of my incorrect diet during
pregnancy and while breastfeeding, and I am
convinced that without constant observation and
immediate action, Alexandra would have been a cot
death statistic.

A couple of years later, I was introduced to Dr
Oliver Lawrence, the greatest naturopath of the
twentieth century. I took Alexandra to see Dr
Lawrence who, after taking one look at her face,
diagnosed dietetic problems. He informed me that
Alexandra's diet was wrong for her and that I
should stop feeding her on cheese, avocado,
bananas and honey. He then turned to look at me
and proceeded to list the foods that I had been
indulging in for the past two years – in particular

dairy produce – which had exaggerated Alexandra's excess mucus condition. I was impressed and astonished by this amazing man and, having already learned a little about naturopathy, eager to explore his diagnostic skills.

Dr Lawrence had trained as a plastic surgeon, but after being cured of an 'incurable' liver disease by the famous English naturopath, A. J. Badham, Dr Lawrence decided that naturopathy was the way forward. He invited Dr Badham to his clinic in South Africa and together they opened a naturopathic teaching school. There I witnessed remarkable healing that filled me with awe and I became Dr Lawrence's devout disciple. Hungry for the knowledge that he had acquired during his sixty years of practice, I enrolled in his School of Naturopathy and studied under the great master himself for three years.

My greatest memories of Dr Lawrence are of his ability to diagnose conditions and dietary imbalances by looking at his patient's face. He was practising a basic form of facial analysis and it is this technique that I have come to use daily with my patients and that – as you will discover for yourself – produces the most amazing results.

I have now been practising naturopathy for over twenty years, most recently at the prestigious Hale Clinic in London, and in that time I have helped literally hundreds of people to regain their vitality and wellbeing by advising them to make simple changes in their daily diet. The facial analysis techniques that I have developed over the years are easy to learn and apply to yourself at home, yet they have the power to transform your health for ever. With this book you will learn to unlock the secrets of your face and find the diet that will make you feel slimmer, happier and healthier than you've ever been!

PART ONE
Introducing Facial Analysis

Naturopathy and the Principles of Facial Analysis

Naturopathy is a nature-based medical system that works to restore and preserve our body's health by treating the cause of the illness or allergy and not the symptom. Naturopathy works in harmony with the body's own natural healing processes and does not rely on drugs, but instead corrects the body's mineral deficiencies through diet, rest and mineral salt supplementation.

Diagnosis may be made through various methods including pulse readings, iridology (examining the iris of the eye), tongue analysis (in Part Three you will find instructions on how you can carry out your own tongue analysis), nail analysis and, most importantly here, facial analysis.

Based on German theories that draw on the principles of biochemistry – the scientific study of the chemical processes that occur in all living organisms – facial analysis is a technique used to detect certain food intolerances as well as digestive problems caused by mineral deficiencies. It is an accurate diagnostic tool which is a key factor in the treatment of disease. It's not difficult – we have all practised it at some stage; puffy eyes, dark rings and paleness of cheeks are all familiar signs of an imbalance of some kind.

Facial analysis is a technique whereby the condition of our body's inner organs can be read and diagnosed by studying the face. Patches of colour, markings, lines, pigmentation and wrinkles are all signs of an imbalance of essential minerals (I'll come on to these a little later on). The fingernails, hands, feet and tongue can also be used as diagnostic tools – after all, years ago the family doctor would ask you to stick out your tongue before examining any other part of the anatomy. But why do the signs of imbalance manifest themselves through the skin? And why the face?

The face is a particularly sensitive part of the anatomy and is affected by many fluctuations within the body. It is the lack of one or more of the essential minerals that create abnormal conditions from within which manifest outwardly through the face. When the appropriate minerals are administered, health is restored. If the minerals are not replaced, severe allergies and/or illness may occur.

Many people think that disease occurs overnight but in fact depletion of these essential minerals occurs over many years. The body is the most miraculous machine ever made and can withstand years of abuse before finally dying. The body is equipped with an alarm system that screams for help when disease attacks. It is when we choose to ignore these signals that the cells have a complete breakdown and 'crisis' ensues.

Facial analysis is a personalized therapy, involving a knowledge of how the action of the minerals within you affect your own health. It will teach you how to recognize your body's signals and avert a crisis.

What will facial analysis do for me?

People come to me for a variety of different reasons. These can vary from a desire to be free of long-standing skin complaints like eczema or acne, to treat persistent headaches and allergies, or because they are experiencing a general feeling of tiredness and lethargy. However I would estimate that the majority of my patients come in order to lose weight. And, as you will see, they do indeed lose weight on this programme – fast. And so will you!

Each of the individual Face Type Plans and the Core Diet have been designed to carefully balance

13

the minerals in the body, which affect our metabolic rate. An over-indulgence in certain foods may deplete one of the minerals thereby causing an imbalance in the others. This in turn affects how fast our body burns up fat and it also has an impact on our energy levels.

In addition to achieving your ideal weight you can also expect to see the following:

☆ Your nails will become stronger and healthier

☆ Your skin will become opaque and even in tone and texture

☆ Dry patches of skin will disappear completely

☆ The whites of your eyes will become much whiter

☆ Your hair will become glossy and shiny and incredibly strong

☆ Lines and wrinkles will soften and, in some cases, disappear completely

☆ You will experience a surge in energy and vitality

☆ You will find that you have become more tolerant and patient

☆ Your mind will be clear and your memory vastly improved

☆ Food will no longer be the highlight of your day, but will be enjoyed at the time of each meal

☆ Problems with digestion will disappear

☆ Those cheekboones you never knew you had will appear

☆ Your confidence will grow

But don't just take my word for it. The following case histories – all true! – show how facial analysis can help to diagnose the underlying causes of all sorts of problems, from unexplained weight gain to infertility.

One patient who comes to mind is a young woman called Valerie. She looks like a young Doris Day and she has a tendency to put on excess weight. She was 21 years old, 5'5" tall and weighed 13 stone. She also suffered from chronic eczema and under doctor's orders had been applying hydrocortisone cream to her face, neck, arms and chest for twenty years. She was four stone overweight, bloated, lethargic, and she suffered from acute pre-menstrual syndrome. I explained that eating the wrong foods as a small child and continuing the same diet throughout her adolescence was the cause of her maladies. I noted that Valerie had a bluish/whitish look in a half circle under her eyes and also that her face was pale. This indicated that she was lacking in the mineral salt that controls allergies: Kali-muir. Her facial analysis also revealed that she was lacking in essential vitamins and minerals, in particular vitamin A and zinc (without zinc, vitamin A cannot be absorbed).

15

It also showed that her liver was sluggish, which was contributing to her lethargy and weight retention. The liver is the largest single organ in the body, filling the top right-hand part of the abdomen, and it plays a crucial role in digestion.

Valerie's diet consisted of chocolate, pickles, cheese, milk, cakes, bread, pasta, mayonnaise and marmalade. I changed her diet to include foods such as kelp, artichokes, chicory, leeks, onion, potatoes, apples, apricots, squash, goat's cheese and carob. Valerie lost four stone on the diet within a matter of months and, perhaps even more importantly, her skin is now blemish-free – *without* the use of artificial steroids and their accompanying unpleasant side-effects. That was four years ago and Valerie boasts beautiful skin and is very happy with her new dress size 10.

Another person who made an enormous change to their health with the Facial Analysis Diet was a middle-aged man called James. James is a six-foot-two policeman who came to see me because his wife was complaining about his rather large stomach! James is a diabetic and according to his doctor should accept his extra load as part of his disease. During his facial analysis I ascertained that his thyroid was sluggish (his eyes were rather protruding). The thyroid is the butterfly-shaped gland which crosses the windpipe just below the Adam's apple, and its function is to control metabolism and body growth. I also noticed that he had dark rings underneath his eyes which indicated a shortage of oxygen. I prescribed the minerals Ferr-phos and Kali-phos to correct this and to improve James's energy level and to enable him to cope with his change of diet. during the consultation I could see that James's face had a yellow/greenish hue and that his tongue was thick and furry which suggested that his liver was sluggish. James was a model patient and swapped his diet of beer, pasta and bread for one including green beans, potatoes, onion, garlic and white wine. He lost an incredible three stone in only six weeks. But more importantly, he also found that he could cut back on his insulin intake for the first time in fifteen years.

Susie was utterly exhausted when she first came to see me. She was bloated, lethargic, moody and one and a half stone overweight. She had an eighteen-month-old baby and despite trying numerous different diets she could not shed the excess pounds she had gained during her pregnancy. During her facial analysis, I noticed that her pancreas was not working at its optimum level. The pancreas is the organ that produces the digestive juices necessary for breaking down the food that we eat, as well as producing the hormones glucagon and insulin, which regulate the glucose levels in the bloodstream. She was also

17

lacking zinc, the great mineral balancer without which the body is unable to absorb other minerals. I prescribed various vitamins and minerals including the homeopathic Zincum 6 and changed her diet according to her facial signs. Within six weeks, Susie had lost one and a half stone and at last looked and felt like her old self.

It's not only individuals who benefit from facial analysis – sometimes couples come to see me together. Jane and Michael were one such young couple, who were desperate for a second child. They had one son, Alexander, aged eight, but were having great difficulty in conceiving again. Jane complained of fluctuating weight gain, bloating and chocolate cravings. They had been trying for another baby for two years, during which time Jane had miscarried. Jane informed me that she had consulted several specialists, who had confirmed that her only chance of conceiving again would be through IVF treatment, because Michael's sperm was immobile.

Jane was reluctant to try IVF treatment and decided to seek alternative advice. During my interview with Jane, I ascertained that although she was ovulating, her periods were non-existent, and this had been the case for several months. I changed her diet and prescribed herbs to regulate her menstrual cycle, according to her facial analysis. I also administered essential minerals.

Within a couple of months, Jane's period returned.

When Michael came to see me, his facial analysis revealed that he had too much acid in his diet and that his liver was sluggish. He confirmed this by informing me that most days he awoke from a deep sleep feeling unrested. His facial signs indicated that he had been taking medication over a period of time. These drugs would have been absorbed after the conception of his first child, which would explain his sperm change from mobility to immobility.

On reflection, Michael revealed that for the last few years he had participated in a course of injections recommended by his GP to protect him from the hazards of the English winter. I suggested he stop the injections forthwith and I prescribed homeopathic remedies to withdraw the harmful side-effects of the drugs. I also modified his diet (banning him from chocolate as he is a self-confessed chocaholic), and administered a combination of vitamins and minerals.

Within three months I was delighted to hear that Jane was pregnant and their baby girl was born later that year without complications. Within six months, Jane had lost all her baby weight and regained her slim figure.

So, now you have seen how the Facial Analysis Diet has transformed the lives of my patients, let's see how it can work for you.

19

Understanding the
Twelve Mineral Salts

Before you can enjoy all the benefits of the Facial
Analysis Diet, it is important to understand what I
mean when I refer to the twelve mineral salts, as
these will play an important role in your diet plan.
So what *are* the essential minerals that are so
imperative for our wellbeing? They were first
identified in Germany in the nineteenth century by
Dr Wilhelm Heinrich Schuessler, a doctor of
medicine, chemistry and physics. Dr Schuessler
began the study of homeopathy as a student and
made some extraordinary discoveries in his study
of biochemic tissue salts. He found that the body
needs twelve essential mineral salts (also known as
tissue salts) for daily function and maintenance.

These twelve mineral salts are the material
basis of the organs and tissues and are essential to
their structure and foundation, as well as being

vital to the correct function of human cells. Our bodies produce these salts naturally, but traces are found in the fruit and vegetables that we eat, since the mineral salts originate from the earth's crust. However, pollution and the misuse of fertilizers and pesticides strip our natural foods of these salts which results in our bodies absorbing insufficient quantities.

A deficiency of these minerals will be carried over from a mother, during pregnancy, to her child (just as allergies – like my own dairy intolerance – can be carried over). If the minerals are not replaced in sufficient quantities, the body draws from its own resources and becomes unable to defend itself against degenerative diseases.

It was Dr Schuessler's followers who established the Facial Analysis Theory, which was first published in 1936. Dr Schuessler and his colleagues correlated every known disease during their research. They studied the faces of their patients and noted that the lines, pigmentation, markings and colourings on their faces corresponded with certain diseases. Scientific trials were carried out over many years, and it was noted that when the patient was given the appropriate mineral the symptoms revealed on the face would become softer or disappear altogether.

Facial analysis is a concept that everybody has practised at some time during their life. Pale

21

cheeks, puffy eyes, dark rings and yellow skin colourings are familiar signs. The principal advantage of facial analysis is the early detection of changes taking place within the inner organs and the correction of the problem in its acute stage before it becomes chronic. Acute disease is self-eliminating if corrected in time: in other words, the disease burns itself out when the toxic matter causing the 'crisis' has been consumed. Chronic disease occurs when an acute disease is neglected or wrongly treated, and it can be life-threatening.

A lack of essential minerals will cause the immune system to weaken which will lead to a sluggish metabolism and, if left unchecked, serious allergies will occur. To combat a deficiency, mineral salts may be supplemented in tablet form – all twelve are readily available at health food shops and chemists. When the 'salt' is placed in the mouth, the powder dissolves and the invisible energy radicals are freed. Once absorbed, they enter the bloodstream and are carried to where they are needed most.

I have listed the twelve mineral salts below, giving their proper name first and their more common name – which I will refer to throughout – in brackets.

1. Calcium Fluoride (Calc Fluor)
2. Calcium Phosphorus (Calc Phos)

3. Calcium Sulphate (Calc Sulph)
4. Iron Phosphate (Ferr Phos)
5. Potassium Chloride (Kali Muir)
6. Potassium Phosphate (Kali Phos)
7. Potassium Sulphate (Kali Sulph)
8. Magnesium Phosphate (Mag Phos)
9. Sodium Chloride (Nat Muir)
10. Sodium Phosphate (Nat Phos)
11. Sodium Sulphate (Nat Sulph)
12. Silica Oxide (Silica)

Each of the twelve mineral salts perform specific functions in balancing and strengthening your body. Every one of us will respond in slightly different ways to any imbalance or deficiency, and it is by studying your face that you may ascertain exactly what it is that your body requires. It is then a simple matter of correcting the imbalance by taking the right mineral salt (or salts) and by following a diet that is right for you.

Which of the twelve mineral salts are you lacking in your diet?

Before I show you how to read your own facial signs and for you to see which of the six diets is right for you, here is a brief outline of the function of each of the twelve mineral salts and the facial signs that indicate a deficiency of each salt. Other

23

signs of a deficiency may also be identified elsewhere in the body and in our behaviour.

Calc Fluor

Function of the mineral salt

☆ Calc Fluor is the connective tissue mineral and is also responsible for good strong teeth

☆ It is the elastic fibre tissue salt that is responsible for healthy elasticity. Without the correct balance of Calc Fluor, the skin will become flabby and loose and stretch marks will appear.

☆ Elastic fibres are not only found in the skin but also in the bone joint capsules, tooth coating and the alimentary tract. The correct amount of this mineral in the system is necessary for good bowel movements

☆ Calcium Fluoride is normally found in water, however in many countries the amounts necessary are scarce. In this case supplementation of Calc Fluor is necessary otherwise the body robs from within – from areas such as the skin (leaving it dry and cracked) or the tooth coating (leaving the teeth stained brown)

Facial signs of a deficiency
☆ Brownish/reddish marking around eyes especially in the corners above and below lids
☆ Dry flaky skin

Further signs of a deficiency
☆ Dry and cracked heels
☆ Dry elbows
☆ Constipation
☆ Hard calluses under feet
☆ Flabby stomach and stretch marks

Calc Phos

Function of the mineral salt
☆ Calc Phos is the cell restorer and nutritive mineral found in bones and teeth. When teeth crumble it is because there is a shortage of this mineral
☆ Calc Phos aids a speedy recovery to people who are convalescing
☆ It is an excellent remedy for young girls suffering from heavy periods as it combats anaemia
☆ It promotes growth in young children, because of its importance to the soft growing tissue
☆ Women suffer a greater deficiency of Calc Phos than men. One of the reasons is that

25

when a woman is pregnant her need for Calc Phos is a major requirement for the developing embryo. If the need is not met in the diet then the body will draw the baby's needs from the mother's own resources and this could leave the mother suffering with teeth problems

Facial signs of a deficiency
☆ Pale and waxy complexion
☆ Soft teeth
☆ Gaunt look about face

Further signs of a deficiency
☆ Introversion in children
☆ Numbness
☆ Palpitations
☆ Melancholia and tearfulness
☆ Delayed bone healing or osteoporosis
☆ Tickly cough with no mucus

Calc Sulph

Function of the mineral salt
☆ This mineral has a good relationship with Silica because they are both excellent for purifying the blood
☆ Calc Sulph removes waste products from the blood and cleanses and purifies the entire system

Facial signs of a deficiency

☆ Severe adult acne
☆ Pustules (with a thick, creamy mucus)

Further signs of a deficiency

☆ A lack of this mineral delays the removal of decaying matter, resulting in boils, carbuncles and abscesses
☆ Excess mucus and catarrh in the lungs and bronchioles

Ferr Phos

Function of the mineral salt

☆ Ferr Phos is a catalyst for iron; it is found in the blood and in the hair. The body only absorbs the iron when it is required
☆ It is essential for young girls with heavy periods
☆ Ferr Phos is an excellent oxygen carrier. Oxygen deprivation can be caused by burdening the body with excess stress, both physical and mental
☆ This mineral is nature's anti-inflammatory. Coupled with Kali Phos it is excellent for lowering fevers
☆ Ferr Phos is an immune-system booster and should be the first line of defence for colds, flu and bacterial infections

27

☆ This is an excellent supplement for children who have an adverse attitude to green vegetables

Facial signs of deficiency
☆ Flushed, red complexion
☆ Dark shadows under the eyes
☆ Flushed, red ears

Further signs of a deficiency
☆ Immune deficiency – frequent colds and flu
☆ Bacterial infections
☆ Tiredness
☆ Shortness of breath
☆ Bleeding
☆ Vascular pain, headaches behind the eyes
☆ Constipation with a burning sensation in the rectum due to dry faeces, which may cause symptoms such as piles (haemorrhoids) and a prolapsed rectum

Kali Muir

Function of the mineral salt
☆ Kali Muir is a blood conditioner and detoxifier
☆ It is found in the muscles, nerves and brain cells. No new brain cell formation can take place without this salt
☆ It is necessary for blood clotting

☆ Kali Muir is the chief remedy for spasmodic croup

☆ Kali Muir should be taken to treat all skin diseases that manifest in blisters (chicken pox, herpes – both simplex and genital – and shingles)

☆ It should be taken in alternation with Ferr Phos in all catarrhal conditions

☆ It is excellent for catarrh in the Eustachian tube (the tube that leads from the middle ear to the throat), which, when blocked, causes temporary hearing loss

☆ Light-coloured stools (due to a lack of bile) is a sign of sluggishness of the liver and this indicates a great need of Kali Muir

Facial signs of a deficiency

☆ Whitish/blueish hue on area around the eyes, often on the upper or lower lids

☆ White face

☆ Glandular swellings

☆ A white, sticky mucus exuding from the eyes

☆ Swollen and painful cheeks

☆ Grey coating on the tongue

Further signs of a deficiency

☆ Warts

☆ Nausea, especially morning sickness during pregnancy

☆ Thick white discharge exuding from anywhere on the body
☆ Allergies

Kali Phos

Function of the mineral salt

☆ Kali Phos is a nerve nutrient and is excellent for students who are studying for exams and who find that concentration eludes them
☆ It is a constituent of all the tissues and fluids of the body, notably the brain, nerves and muscles
☆ This tissue salt is necessary for the oxidation processes (the transformation of gases in respiration)

Facial signs of a deficiency

☆ Brownish coating to tongue
☆ Tongue sticking to roof of the mouth

Further signs of a deficiency

☆ Mental anxiety
☆ Pessimistic attitude
☆ Slowness of the brain
☆ Poor memory
☆ Mental and physical exhaustion
☆ Procrastination is one of the most obvious symptoms of a deficiency. This indicates a

sluggish mind and a tired mental state, usually
following great mental strain

Kali Sulph

Function of the mineral salt
☆　This mineral salt is found in the intercellular
fluids, nerves, muscles, epithelium and the
blood
☆　It is an oxygen carrier
☆　It is also an important kidney toner and
conditioner. This is essential during
pregnancy as the kidneys are overworked
filtering out the extra fluids. This is why more
women than men are deficient in this mineral
☆　Kali Sulph is the main remedy for the skin

Facial signs of a deficiency
☆　Oil, greasy skin with yellowish eruptions
☆　Brownish/yellow face colour
☆　Dry scalp with yellow scales
☆　Dandruff
☆　Slimy, yellow-coated tongue

Further signs of a deficiency
☆　Kali Sulph, like Ferr Phos, is an oxygen carrier.
Deficiency in this mineral can result in
discoloration of the skin, particularly a bronze
appearance
☆　Strong desire for fresh air

31

☆ Inflammatory pain
☆ Age spots on hands and face

Mag Phos

Function of the mineral salt

☆ Mag Phos is an anti-spasmodic painkiller
☆ An imbalance of this mineral causes the muscles to contract, causing cramps, bone pain and paralysis (the opposite of Ferr Phos which causes muscles to relax)
☆ This cell salt is mostly confined to the white nerve fibres of the nerves and muscles
☆ An imbalance of this mineral causes migraine and interrupted vision because of the spasmodic condition of blood vessels that feed the retina. Sparks or colours may be seen in front of the eyes

Facial signs of deficiency

☆ Lean and thin body
☆ Red area around the nose
☆ Flushed face

Further signs of a deficiency

☆ Highly nervous disposition
☆ Muscle cramps
☆ Bloatedness

☆ Teething pains in babies
☆ Hot flushes
☆ Sharp, shooting, darting neuralgic pains
☆ Migraine

Nat Muir

Function of the mineral salt
☆ Nat Muir is Sodium Chloride, but do not think
of this mineral as you would think of common
table salt, because the micro-molecular
structure of Nat Muir has the reverse effect.
Common salt draws water towards it, causing
oedema (an excessive accumulation of fluids),
whereas Nat Muir shifts water to wherever
moisture is needed

Facial signs of a deficiency
☆ A silvery line underneath the eyelashes
☆ Bloated face
☆ Puffiness underneath the eyes
☆ Sponginess of cheeks

Further signs of a deficiency
☆ Nat Muir controls the amount of hydrochloric
acid necessary for digestion. Without this
mineral digestive disturbances would arise
because of too little acid

☆ Any swelling in the body
☆ Dry, itchy skin
☆ Discharge from anywhere in the body of a clear, watery mucus
☆ Watery blisters

Nat Phos

Function of the mineral salt

☆ This mineral salt is present in the blood, nerves, muscles, brain cells and intercellular fluids
☆ Nat Phos regulates the correct balance of acid within the body by splitting lactic acid into carbonic acid and water. (Excess acid in the tissues causes arthritis and rheumatism and also has an adverse effect on the digestion.)
☆ This mineral also eliminates excess water from the body. It is quite distinct from the other two water-regulating minerals, Nat Muir and Nat Sulph.

Facial signs of a deficiency

☆ Small amounts of golden yellow mucus stuck to eyelids on waking
☆ Tongue coated a creamy yellow
☆ Large pores, or
☆ Tight pores

Further signs of a deficiency

☆ Coppery taste in the mouth

☆ Heart burn

☆ Stiffness and rheumatic conditions around the joints (especially in the ankles, toes, elbows and fingers)

☆ Burning sensation on the skin

☆ Constipation

☆ Cravings for sweets and starches

☆ Smelly feet

Nat Sulph

Function of the mineral salt

☆ Nat Sulph regulates the amount of water in the tissues

☆ It also assists the liver in keeping bile the correct consistency

Facial signs of a deficiency

☆ Greenish/yellowish colouring on the face

☆ Bluish, reddish nose

☆ Strong, vertical lines between the eyes, above the nose

☆ Furry tongue

☆ Yellow whites of the eyes

Further signs of a deficiency

☆ Hay fever
☆ Liver problems
☆ Sick headaches accompanied by giddiness
☆ Sensitive scalp which is painful when combing hair
☆ Nausea

Silica

Function of the mineral salt

☆ Silica is present in the blood, bile, hair, nails and skin
☆ It is a constituent of connective tissue and of the mucous membrane
☆ This mineral is necessary for a strong nervous system. (An easy diagnostic test is to sit in traffic during rush hour and note how close to the edge you are. If you feel like screaming or bashing everyone on the head, you most likely have a shortage of this mineral!)

Facial signs of a deficiency

☆ A shiny bald head
☆ A glossy nose tip
☆ Brownish tongue
☆ A polished, shiny forehead
☆ Dull, fluffy hair

☆ Hard lumps underneath the skin (not suppurating)

Further signs of a deficiency
☆ Aggressiveness
☆ Irritation and lack of concentration in children
☆ Sensitivity to light and noise
☆ Falling hair

Now that you have been introduced to the twelve mineral salts and the ways in which they affect us, it's time to move on to the six face types. In this section you will be learning how to discover for yourself which type you are, before moving on to the appropriate diet plan in Part Two.

The Six Face Types and How to Identify Yourself

We are all unique and we all have different nutritional and mineral requirements, but each one of us will fall into one of six main 'types'. Each type will display a combination of particular facial signs that are unique to that type only.

As you read through the six descriptions below there may be facial signs belonging to more than one type that apply to you. Don't worry! This is not unusual – we are all incredibly sensitive to mineral and nutritional imbalances and we will, at varying times, display a combination of symptoms.

Working out your own particular face type may take a bit of time and concentration, so don't panic if it doesn't become apparent right away. The descriptions below and the diagrams on pages 41 to 50 are a guide, but we are all different so you shouldn't expect your own facial signs to mirror exactly those in the diagrams. Nor should you expect to display *all* the facial signs and other complaints listed within your type description.

It may help to have a friend with you when working out your face type. We're all so used to looking at our own faces that sometimes it's easy to overlook certain signs, particularly colourings. A friend will help you to see yourself objectively.

Remove all traces of make-up and position yourself squarely in front of a large mirror. If you have long hair, it may help to tie it back. Make sure that your face is well lit with a bright light. Then take time to study your *entire* face, noting the different colours, tones, pigmentation, lines and pore sizes. It may feel a bit strange at first but just concentrate and take your time.

Look at each section of the face: the hairline, the fore-head, the eyes (both above and below), the nose and the creases around the nose, the cheeks and the chin and jaw.

Then, look at the diagrams on pages 41 to 50 and carefully read through the descriptions below. Make a mark or tick next to those facial signs listed that apply to you. Don't worry at this stage if you tick off the signs that belong to more than one type.

Spend some time doing this, then take a break, have a stretch. When you're ready, go back to your mirror and see if there's anything that you have missed off the first time round. Repeat the procedure above, carefully reading through the descriptions and again making a mark against any of the signs that you have missed.

Then move on to the 'other complaints' description and again, mark off which of these most apply to you.

Finally, tally up the number of ticks by each type. By this stage you will find that there will be one description of a type by which you have placed the most ticks. This is the type with which you *most* identify, over and above the remaining five.

Introducing the face types

Type A

General description

The symptoms and facial signs of Type A are largely caused by the thyroid gland. This small gland lies in front of the windpipe and produces the hormone thyroxine. Thyroxine regulates the body's metabolism and determines the level of activity within the body. If the level of thyroxine is too high the individual will become hyperactive (hyper-thyroidism) and lose weight rapidly. If, however, the thyroxine level is too low (hypothyroidism) the

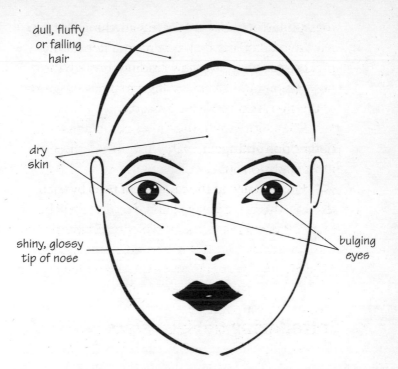

dull, fluffy or falling hair

dry skin

shiny, glossy tip of nose

bulging eyes

individual will become lethargic, unmotivated and, on occasion, obese. This latter type may also suffer from thinning hair, dryness of skin (especially the hands), cold feet and unexplained weight gain.

Depending on whether you have an over- or under-active thyroid gland you may show signs of hyperactivity or sluggishness respectively.

The facial signs
☆ Shiny, glossy tip of nose
☆ Dull, fluffy or falling hair

41

☆ Bulging eyes – usually a personal or hereditary characteristic, however when the eyes become suddenly more pronounced or fixed in a stare, the common cause is an over-active thyroid

☆ Dryness of skin

Other complaints

☆ Occasionally a swelling in the neck

☆ Cold hands and feet

☆ Dry skin, especially the hands

Type B

General description

Type Bs are ruled by the liver. The liver is the body's detoxifying machine filtering out toxins. But if the liver becomes blocked and overloaded due to poor diet or, in certain cases, the taking of medication, the body becomes tired and sluggish and this is often accompanied by a feeling of depression or moodiness.

Type Bs have a tendency to produce too much bile in the body's attempt to restore the balance upset by the clogged liver, which in turn prompts a desire for sugar and sweet foods. The consumption of sweets and chocolate triggers a vicious cycle, further clogging up the liver, worsening the mood and leading to yet more cravings. And so the liver –

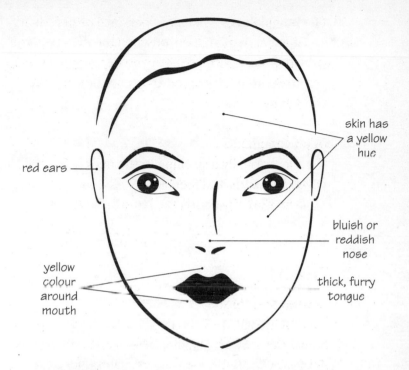

red ears

skin has a yellow hue

bluish or reddish nose

yellow colour around mouth

thick, furry tongue

rather than the heart – is very much the emotional organ of the body. Chewing lemon rind will quash any sugar cravings, strengthen your liver and help to rebalance the emotions.

The facial signs
☆   Yellow hue to the skin
☆   Bluish or reddish nose
☆   Red ears
☆   Yellow colour around the mouth
☆   Furry, thick tongue

43

Other complaints

☆ Awakening from a deep sleep feeling exhausted

☆ Lack of motivation and concentration

☆ Feeling of nausea

Type C

General description

If you are a Type C, you will notice that your body often becomes 'waterlogged', particularly in the hands, feet, ankles and legs. You may feel that your body puffs up at times, even when you otherwise feel in perfect health, although you are more likely to experience this sensation after a long flight, or, if you are a woman, during menstruation.

Try pressing the trouble spot with your thumb. If an indentation remains – instead of the tissue springing back – you are most likely suffering from oedema. Oedema is a sign of an overloaded system and like any other overload it should be drained by moving the excess liquid from the main organs into the extremities. This can be done by following a correct diet and, if necessary, taking the appropriate vitamins and minerals.

The causes of oedema are many, including varicose veins, kidney and liver starvation, under-active thyroid and medication. The best treatment is to cut down on salt and to drink at least 2 litres of

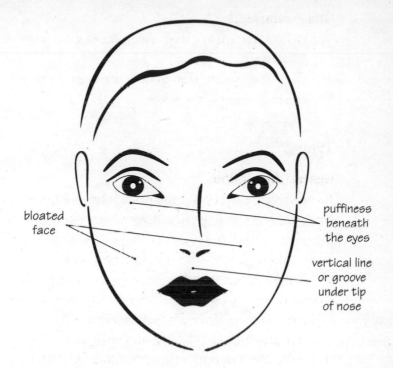

bloated face

puffiness beneath the eyes

vertical line or groove under tip of nose

water daily. The diet should consist of freshly steamed vegetables and green leafy salads. Red meat should be avoided and fish limited because of the high mercury and salt content.

The facial signs

☆ Puffiness beneath the eyes

☆ A bloated face

☆ There may be a vertical line or groove under the tip of the nose

45

Other complaints

☆ Swollen ankles

☆ Swollen fingers

☆ A lack of concentration (this is caused by too much water on the brain)

Type D

General description

In general, Type Ds may be prone to rheumatism or arthritis or perhaps may have parents or even

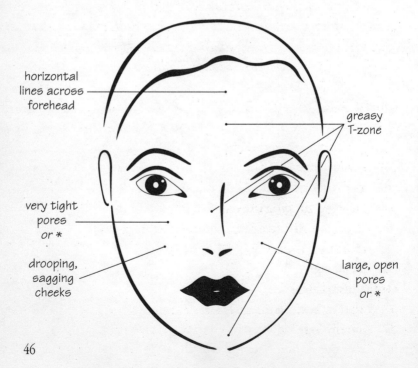

horizontal lines across forehead

greasy T-zone

very tight pores or *

drooping, sagging cheeks

large, open pores or *

grandparents who have suffered from these conditions. Rheumatism is a chronic inflammatory condition that can affect the whole body, which is why it's all the more important to ensure you have the correct diet so as to avoid the terrible pain of this illness.

In some cases Type Ds may display inflammation on the body, often manifesting as painful and burning red lumps or abscesses which may be aggravated by damp surroundings and an excess of sugar or alcohol.

The Type D personality may be rather rigid with a tendency towards perfectionism. There may be a great need to keep everything in its proper place, lest they become too overwhelmed!

The facial signs
☆ Greasy T-zone (this is the T-shaped area of the forehead, nose and chin)
☆ Large, open pores, or
☆ Very tight pores
☆ Droopy, sagging cheeks
☆ Horizontal lines across forehead (this can indicate a digestion problem)

Other complaints
☆ Acid reflux, particularly after eating
☆ Smelly feet

Type E

General description

Type Es are particularly intolerant of dairy products and a combination of a poor diet and stress will often cause eczema or psoriasis. Eczema is an itchy inflammatory skin condition which starts with small dry patches around the eyes and nose and spreads to the face, wrists and creases of the elbows and knees. Foods that exacerbate the condition include strawberries, mangoes, dates, bananas and eggs.

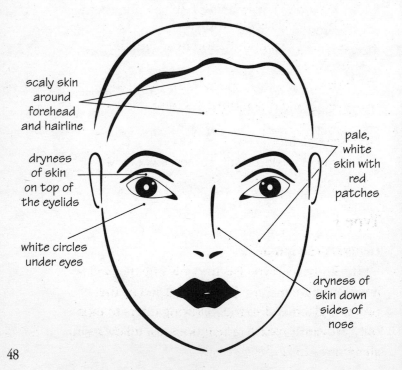

scaly skin around forehead and hairline

dryness of skin on top of the eyelids

white circles under eyes

pale, white skin with red patches

dryness of skin down sides of nose

Type Es often display a bluish or reddish colouration on the lower and upper eyelids indicating a chronic storage of Potassium Chloride (Kali Muir). They should make sure they are getting plenty of Vitamins B and C.

Type Es tend to be worriers – exacerbated by a lack of Vitamin B. They are also great food lovers, so they need to watch that they are not over-indulging.

The facial signs
☆　Pale, white skin with red patches
☆　White circles under the eyes
☆　Scaly skin around the forehead and the hairline
☆　Dryness of skin, especially on top of the eyelids and down the sides of the nose

Other complaints
☆　Dryness of skin in all creases, e.g. elbows or knees

Type F

General description
Of the six types, Type F is the only one that will *not* apply to women. Type Fs are governed by the prostate gland and so the following refers to men only. However please note it does not follow that all men will be Type F.

49

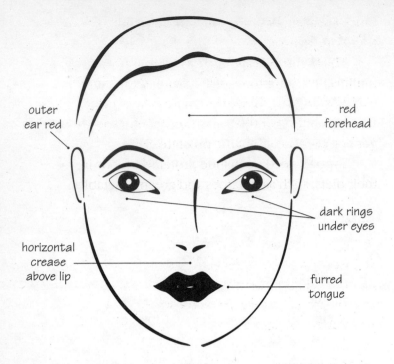

outer
ear red

red
forehead

dark rings
under eyes

horizontal
crease
above lip

furred
tongue

The prostate gland, which is located in the neck of the bladder in men, can occasionally be the source of a variety of problems – the most common being cystitis. When this occurs the urethra is squeezed and urinating becomes difficult. With partial flow urine backs up into the kidneys and stagnates, creating a haven for bacteria and infection. A raised temperature and a burning sensation when urinating is a sign that all is not well. A change in diet and plenty of water is essential for recovery. Beer, coffee, pepper and soy sauce are all aggravating foods and should therefore be avoided.

The herb Saw Palmetto has been shown to diminish the symptoms of an inflamed prostate gland by assisting in regulating the flow of urine, while Evening Primrose oil is excellent for the general good health of the prostate gland.

Type Fs need to include protective foods in their diets, such as potatoes and green vegetables.

The facial signs
☆ Red forehead
☆ Red top of the outer ear
☆ Dark rings under the eyes
☆ Horizontal crease above the top lip
☆ Furred tongue

Other complaints
☆ An enlarged prostate gland obstructs the outflow of urine causing discomfort and a frequent desire to pass water. Later the retention of water occurs
☆ General tiredness
☆ A rise in temperature
☆ Thirst
☆ Constipation
☆ Occasional vomiting

51

Well done! You should now have successfully identified your own personal face type and you may move on to the appropriate eating plan found in Part Two.

The Eating Plans

Introducing the
Facial Analysis Diet

You are about to embark on a wonderful and life-enhancing programme! For the next two days you will be following an eating plan tailored *exactly* to your own specific dietary needs and requirements as defined by your own face type.

It is essential that you follow your two-day Face Type Plan *first* before moving on to the two-week Core Diet.

The two-day Face Type Plan works to correct the balance of your body, boost your metabolism, begin to rid your body of the various toxins that have accumulated and provide you with all the correct minerals and nutrients essential for your type and for your wellbeing.

Once you have completed the two-day plan you should then move on to the Core Diet which covers two weeks. You may find that one week is

55

sufficient or that other commitments prevent you from continuing on to the second week, but in general I would advise that you attempt to complete the entire programme.

The two-day Face Type Plan has been carefully devised over my many years of practising facial analysis, so it is very important that you follow it carefully and as strictly as you can!

Getting ready

Timing is essential when embarking on any kind of diet. You can of course begin the Facial Analysis Diet on any day of the week but it will help make the plan easier if you begin it at a time when you have relatively little scheduled, so make sure that you plan ahead. There is no point in starting on your two-day plan the day your in-laws are arriving, or if you have an important business lunch or a heavy week of socializing planned. You may already know how difficult it can be to stick to an eating plan when you have a busy work and social schedule – particularly when it may include eating or drinking out. There is a great temptation in these situations to abandon all good intentions! So try to find a quiet week to begin.

Make time for yourself and, if it helps, let those around you know – tell your friends, your spouse and your children that you'll be preparing separate meals for yourself. Try to avoid putting yourself into situations where you may feel pressured to eat and drink foods that aren't permitted over this period.

Scan through the two-day Face Type Plan and make a list of all the foods that you'll need. There are a number of items that you can shop for in advance and you can buy the appropriate fruits and vegetables the day before you begin, to ensure that they are as fresh as possible. (If you have time, I would suggest that you buy fresh organic produce, as and when you need it.)

Specialist foods and supplements

During the course of the two-day Face Type Plan and the two-week Core Diet, you may come across certain foods that are not familiar to you, or foods that you are unable to find in your local supermarket. This is not meant to make the diet tricky for you, but rather to introduce some alternative wholesome, nutritious and extremely filling foods into your diet. For example, you may be used to eating lots of wheat – particularly bread – but wheat can often cause negative side-effects. These alternative foods will help to replace some of the less healthy options in your normal diet.

The following foods are those which you may need to shop for in a specialist health food shop or large supermarket. They are not expensive or hard to cook with and I will be including recipes and instructions on how to use them:

Quinoea   Pronounced 'keenwa', this is a wonderful protein-rich flour that was originally used by the Incas. It is an excellent breakfast food as it is extremely filling and keeps hunger away.

Millet   This alkaline grain is the seed of a fruit. This is another great hunger satisfier and again will form some of your breakfast meals.

Buckwheat pasta   This diet includes very little wheat as it can cause bloating and allergies, but buckwheat is fine and is now used as an alternative to wheat in some pastas.

Morga   This is a yeast- and salt-free alternative to stock made by Bioforce. It is bought in jars and may be found in some health food shops. You may like to add this to soups and sauces for extra flavour, although I have also included a simple stock recipe in Part Four.

Tamari   This is a wheat-free alternative to soy sauce and good for adding to stir fries as it gives extra flavour to cooking.

Bio-salt   Available in health food shops, this contains Potassium Chloride rather than regular salt's Sodium Chloride which is the main cause of water retention and bloatedness.

Organic oat cakes   You can now get organic oat cakes from most supermarkets. If you can, try to buy the variety that contain no salt, sugar or malt. However, don't worry if you can't get completely salt-free oat cakes, as they can be hard to find.

Amaranth biscuits   Amaranth was a sacred food of the Aztecs. A tall plant with broad leaves that produces seeds which are then ground into flour and used in a variety of ways. The biscuits can be found in most health food shops.

Tofuti ice cream   This is a non-dairy ice cream made from tofu and available in the freezer section of health food shops.

Sugar-free jam   This can be found in practically all supermarkets, but do make sure that you don't buy diabetic jam which is full of saccharine.

Herbamare   This is made from 90% organic herbs from Switzerland and 10% organic rock sea salt, and so is a much healthier salt.

Mineral salts   In addition to the diet plans for each type I have also included a suggested supplement of mineral salt (or salts). These can be bought in most health food shops and chemists. They are inexpensive and will help in bringing about the remarkable effects of the Facial Analysis Diet. Take as the manufacturer indicates, usually four tablets on the tongue, three times a day away from meal times.

Important dos and don'ts

The following dos and don'ts apply to all six Face Type Plans *and* to the two-week Core Diet:

☆   Do drink at least two litres of water a day. The body is 75% water and losses through perspiration and urination must be replenished. Water helps to combat obesity, constipation, high blood pressure, skin disease, aches and pains in the joints and it aids digestion. Without water the body's cells die prematurely, so drink plenty for maximum health

☆   Do drink the herbal teas as suggested – but no more than the specified amount

☆   Do eat as much salad and vegetables as you like (as specified for each type) with the exception of spinach where indicated, for

60

which I have included portion size due to its oxalic acid content

☆ Do not add salt or pepper to your food unless specified. Salt attracts water causing bloatedness and water retention while pepper can irritate the inner lining of the stomach. If you must use salt then use Bio-salt and Herbamare (available in health food shops) because this contains Potassium Chloride instead of Sodium Chloride. It is the latter that causes water retention

☆ Don't add sugar to your food unless specified

☆ Don't drink any caffeine during the plan – both coffee and tea can cause headaches, water retention, anxiety and insomnia and greatly affect your concentration

☆ Don't drink any fizzy or diet drinks during the plan

☆ Do avoid all alcohol

☆ Unless stated, do avoid dairy products (with the exception of butter which you will be having lots of!). The protein in lactose (the sugar found in milk) is ten thousand times stronger in cow's milk than in mother's milk. While the calf can tolerate this high protein content because it has a double stomach, we humans cannot

☆ Don't add fat or oil to your cooking unless specified

61

☆ Do try not to switch round your lunch and dinner meals – it is important to avoid going to bed following a heavy meal

☆ Do stick to the suggested meal plans as strictly as you can

☆ Do plan ahead to make the diet easier for yourself – some dried fruits and pulses need soaking overnight, and breakfast breads can be made the previous evening if you are short of time in the mornings

Measuring portions

A brief note about portion sizes. Throughout the individual Face Type Plans and in the Core Diet, I have tried to include precise measurements and quantities. But in the case of certain foods you will need to be your own judge. Remember that your stomach is the size of your fist. Here is a rough guide:

Potatoes   These are a wonderfully filling and nutritious food and you can afford to give yourself a generous portion. Where I have listed a 'large' jacket potato this would probably be the size of your fist – but no bigger.

Fruit   One serving of fruit is the equivalent to one apple, one peach, three plums, three apricots, half a grapefruit, one kiwi fruit, approximately 100g (4 oz) of berries, grapes and cherries, approximately 225g (8 oz) of melon, a medium slice of papaya or one pear.

Salads and vegetables   You may have as much as you like of the salads and vegetables included in the plans (with the exception of potatoes). However this doesn't mean you should eat so much that you feel uncomfortable. A great and transforming aspect of the Facial Analysis Diet is that your relationship with food will change. Meals will no longer be the focus of your day, cravings will subside, and you will not feel hungry after the first two days. So although some foods are 'unlimited' this does not mean you should attempt to eat as many of them as you can. Your body will tell you when you have had enough – so it is important that you pay attention to it.

Where I have given measurements in cup size the equivalent to 1 cup is approximately 225 grams or 8 ounces (or 300 ml or ½ pint of liquid).

Cooking

In order to limit the amount of fat in your diet and to ensure that your meals are tasty and flavourful, you will be cooking in a variety of ways.

Roasting   This applies mostly to vegetables and chicken. Although roasting takes slightly longer than grilling, the results are incredibly tasty and succulent.

Dry frying   Rather than frying in butter or oil you can use a little water when frying to prevent your vegetables sticking.

Steaming   Steamed vegetables taste wonderful and because they are not submerged in boiling water they retain their vitamin content.

Soothing and irritating foods

In addition to the individual Face Type Plans and the Core Diet eating plans, I have included two lists of foods for each type. The first list is headed Irritating Foods and the second list Soothing Foods. There are a number of both soothing and irritating foods that appear in more than one of the individual Face Type Plans. Although we are all different and have different nutritional requirements there are some foods that we can all benefit from and likewise some that we should all try to avoid.

Irritating foods   For each of the six face types there are a number of specific foods that I have termed Irritating Foods and which should be

avoided, both during the two-day Face Type Plan,
the two-week Core Diet and – if you can – after you
have completed the Facial Analysis Diet altogether.
These are foods that react negatively with your
type, so you may be slightly or very allergic to
them. They will inhibit the success of the overall
diet and will exacerbate existing skin irritations and
digestive disorders. By removing these foods from
your diet, you will be speeding up the elimination
of toxins from your body which in turn will help to
bring about the wonderful changes that this diet
promises.

Soothing foods   For each of the six face types
there are also a number of specific foods that are
highly beneficial for that type and which I have
termed Soothing Foods. When seeing patients, I
sometimes refer to these foods as 'nerve' foods
because they have the effect of calming the body
and mind, and help to curb cravings. Each of the
individual Face Type Plans include these soothing
foods, but you may choose to supplement the diet
with additional foods from this list, or replace
certain fruits or vegetables with alternative
soothing foods. During the two-week Core Diet, do
incorporate your own soothing foods into the plan,
particularly if you're experiencing cravings or
perhaps having a stressful period at work or home.
So make sure that throughout the course of the

65

plan you have plenty of your own soothing foods ready at hand.

Soothing drinks　I have also included a list of drinks – a combination of fruit and vegetables juices and herbal teas – for each type. You may choose to replace the specified herbal teas with a juice or tea appropriate for your type if the teas are not to your taste.

The juices are rich in vitamins and minerals and act as great energy boosters, so they are particularly good to take in the afternoon when you may be feeling a little lethargic and in need of a pick-me-up. You can either use a juicer or a regular blender will work just as well. Do make sure you wash your fruit and vegetables first and, if possible, buy organic.

The teas may require using more than one variety at the same time – just place the correct bags together in a teapot or large mug, pour on hot water and leave to steep for three minutes before drinking. I recommend that you take tea at 11 a.m. and 4 p.m. daily, when your energy levels may be in a need of a boost in between meal times.

Before you start

Please note that you may experience some side effects, depending on how toxic your body is.

Symptoms may include nausea, headaches, abscesses, lethargy and tiredness, and diarrhoea alternating with constipation. These symptoms are a positive sign, so don't be alarmed. It means that the toxins are being eliminated from the body. The toxins that are exuding from the body are the result of the withdrawal symptoms rather than the diet itself. It is the absence of particular foods from your diet during the plan that results in the symptoms and not the inclusion of 'new' foods.

If you can persevere for the first two days, all cravings will disappear. This diet is an individual 'nerve' food diet, hence the amazing feeling of relaxation that you are likely to experience during the second or third day into the diet. The results are well worth it! But do note that severe symptoms should be treated seriously.

The Two-Day Face Type Plans

Type A

Irritating foods
Alfalfa sprouts
All yeast products
Barley
Chocolate
Mango
Nuts
Raisins
Red wine
Rye
Sweet potato
Vinegar
White flour

Soothing foods
Apples
Artichokes
Asparagus
Buckwheat
Butter
Camomile
Celery
Chives
Cucumber
Ginger
Kelp
Oats
Potato
Watercress

Soothing drinks
Camomile and lemon tea
Carrot and parsley juice
Carrot, celery and spinach juice
Rosehip and camomile tea

Mineral salt remedy
Silica
Fucus (this is a homeopathic remedy and *not* a
    mineral salt but can also be easily obtained
    from good chemists and health food shops)

Day one

On rising   One glass of warm water with a thin slice of lemon.

Breakfast   Unleavened buckwheat and quinoea bread: mix 1 tbsp of buckwheat flour or flakes with 1 cup of organic oats and 1 tbsp of quinoea flour or flakes and blend the mixture with a little water until it has reached a thick and creamy consistency. Pour into a large, shallow, ovenproof dish (grease first with unsalted butter) and bake in a warm oven for approximately 20 minutes until golden brown. When cooked, turn it out of the dish onto a plate and spread with unsalted butter.

11 a.m.   Choose one of the following herbal teas: peppermint, camomile, lemon and lime or nettle.

Lunch   Large raw salad made from lettuce (any variety), cucumber, celery and watercress. Top with baby new potatoes that have been steamed with a handful of fresh mint.

4 p.m.   Herbal tea (see above for varieties).

Dinner   Braised or grilled chicken breast (remember to remove the skin first), served with the following roasted vegetables: dulse seaweed, carrots, spring greens, courgettes and asparagus. When cooked, add a knob of unsalted butter to taste.

Day two

On rising   One glass of warm water with a thin slice of lemon.

Breakfast   Unleavened buckwheat and quinoea bread (see recipe on page 108 for cooking instructions). Spread with unsalted butter and top with sliced cucumber and tomato.

11 a.m.   Choose one of the following herbal teas: camomile, valerian or lemon balm.

Lunch   A large jacket potato topped with a knob of unsalted butter, served with a large raw salad of lettuce (any variety), cucumber, celery, watercress, and carrot.

4 p.m.   Herbal tea (see above for varieties).

Dinner   One bowl of thick vegetable soup (see recipe on page 142), followed by a grilled chicken breast cooked with herbs and spices (preferably fresh basil, thyme, rosemary and cardamom), served with braised savoy cabbage, asparagus and courgettes.

Type B

Irritating foods
Alcohol
Avocado
Banana
Blue cheese
Chocolate
Coffee
Curry
Dates
Malt
Mango
Oranges
Peanuts
Raisins
Shellfish
Sweet potato

Tea
White flour

Soothing foods
Apples
Apricots
Artichokes
Asparagus
Buckwheat
Cabbage
Carrots
Cherries
Cucumber
Dandelion leaves
Garlic
Grapefruit
Kale
Leeks
Lemon juice and rind
Lettuce
Lime
Millet
Oats
Onions
Parsley
Peaches
Pears
Peas
Plums

Potato
Prunes
Radish
Spinach
Swiss chard
Watercress

Soothing drinks
Apple and lemon juice
Artichoke juice
Cucumber, carrot and parsley juice
Dandelion and nettle juice
Elderflower juice
Grapefruit juice
Radish juice
Tomato juice
Watercress juice

Mineral salt remedy
Nat Sulph

Day one

On rising   One large glass of warm water with a
thin slice of lemon.

Breakfast   Breakfast millet porridge. Mix 1 cup of
organic oats with 1 tbsp organic millet

flour. Place in a saucepan and add a little water to make a creamy consistency. Bring to the boil and simmer for 15 minutes until soft. The porridge should be light and fluffy – almost like rice. When cooked, add unsalted butter to taste.

11 a.m.   Choose one of the following herbal teas: dandelion or nettle.

Lunch   A large green salad of celery, fresh parsley, carrot and lettuce (any variety). Eat with a large cooked globe artichoke dipped in butter.

4 p.m.   Warm lemon water. Chew on some lemon rind.

Dinner   Poached, grilled or steamed sea bass served with steamed vegetables. Try chopped onion, asparagus, courgettes and Swiss chard.

Day two

On rising   One glass of warm water with a thin slice of lime.

Breakfast Unleavened oat bread: mix 1 cup of organic oats with a little water until it achieves a thick, creamy consistency. Add a pinch of ginger or cinnamon to taste. Pour the mixture into a shallow, greased, ovenproof dish and bake in a warm oven until it is golden brown (approximately 20 minutes). Then turn out of the dish onto a plate and spread with unsalted butter.

Fresh apple tea (see recipe on page 157) may be taken in place of breakfast if dinner was consumed late the previous evening.

11 a.m. Choose one of the following herbal teas: lemon and lime, camomile or peppermint.

Lunch One bowl of thick vegetable soup (see recipe on page142), this time replacing the vegetables with onion, garlic, cabbage, courgette and spinach.

Follow this with a large salad of mixed leafy green vegetables including some or all of the following: dandelion leaves, artichoke, fennel and carrot. Dress with lemon and lime juice mixed with herbs, or freshly squeezed pineapple juice.

Follow with one or two portions of ripe juicy fruit – choose from apples, pineapple or papaya.

4 p.m.   Herbal tea (see above for varieties).

Dinner   Grilled fish – choose from haddock, plaice, dover sole, lemon sole, bream or sea bass. You may only have salmon or tuna if you know that it's mercury free and make sure you buy only fresh, not canned, fish. Top with unsalted butter and chopped, fresh parsley.

Serve with a large portion of steamed green vegetables (such as Brussels sprouts, kale, spring greens, savoy cabbage, spinach and artichoke) and a large braised onion.

Type C

Irritating foods
Aubergine
Banana
Canned fruit
Cheese

Chocolate
Coconut
Dates
Jellied fruits
Margarine
Marmalade
Nuts
Peanuts
Pepper
Processed foods (due to their high salt content)
Pumpkin
Raisins
Red meat
Salt
Salted nuts
Sauces (in general, due to high salt content)
Soy sauce
Sweet potato
Wheat
Yam
Yeast products

Soothing foods
Apples
Apricots
Berries
Broccoli
Cabbage
Carrots

Celeriac
Celery
Cherries
Chives
Collard
Dandelion leaves
Endive
Fish (but avoid all canned fish)
Lentils
Oats
Onions
Papaya
Parsley
Peaches
Peas
Pineapple
Potato
Spinach
Spring greens
Swiss chard
White meat

Soothing drinks

Apple, carrot and mint juice
Carrot, celery, parsley and cabbage juice
Carrot, parsley and mint juice
Nettle, dandelion and carrot juice
Watercress, parsley, celery and carrot juice
Water with a thin slice of lemon or lime   79

Note: Try to drink one glass of a vegetable juice daily.

Mineral salt remedy
Nat Muir
Nat Sulph

Note: You should also cut out any additional salt in your diet.

Day one

On rising   One large glass of warm water with a thin slice of lemon.

Breakfast   Four organic oat cakes topped with slices of cucumber and tomato.

11 a.m.   Choose one of the following herbal teas: equisetum (horsetail) or dandelion.

Lunch   Big chips (see recipe on page 152) topped with garlic butter. Serve with a large salad of green leafy vegetables, including raw onions or chives, lettuce (any variety), cucumber, tomato, carrots and celery.

4 p.m.   Choose one of the following herbal teas: celery and parsley (see recipe on page 156), dandelion or nettle.

Dinner   Chicken breast – grilled, poached or fried with a little water to stop it sticking (do not add oil or fat). Serve with steamed vegetables: asparagus, white cabbage and green beans.

Day two

On rising   One large glass of warm water with a thin slice of lime.

Breakfast   Breakfast porridge: mix 1 cup of organic oats with a little water, bring to the boil and simmer for 15 minutes until thick and creamy. When cooked, add a knob of unsalted butter to add creaminess.

11 a.m.   Choose one of the following herbal teas: nettle or dandelion.

Lunch   A large jacket potato topped with a knob of unsalted butter. Serve with a large raw salad of lettuce (any variety), cucumber, tomato, carrot, celery and watercress.

4 p.m.   Herbal tea (see above for varieties).

Dinner   Grilled turkey breast served with the following steamed vegetables: broccoli, Brussels sprouts, cabbage and asparagus. Top with a knob of unsalted butter.

Type D

Irritating foods

All alcohol

Aubergine

Barley

Bread containing yeast

Chocolate

Dressings

Mango

Marmalade

Mayonnaise

Pasta

Pastry

Pies

Red meat (all)

Rice

Roasted nuts

Shellfish

Soy sauce

Tomato
Vinegar

Soothing foods
Apples
Artichokes
Asparagus
Berries
Cabbage
Carrots
Celery
Chard
Cherries
Cucumber
Dandelion leaves
Endive
Fresh horseradish
Lettuce
Millet
Oats
Quinoea flour and flakes
Turnip

Soothing drinks
Artichoke, celery and dandelion juice
Carrot, parsley and dandelion juice
Carrot and horseradish juice
Celery and horseradish juice

Mineral salt remedy
Nat Phos

Day one

On rising   One glass of warm water with a thin slice of lime.

Breakfast   Breakfast porridge: mix 1 cup of organic oats with a little water, bring to the boil and simmer until soft and creamy (approximately 15 minutes). When cooked, add a knob of unsalted butter to taste.

11 a.m.   Choose one of the following herbal teas: nettle, dandelion, birch leaf or parsley.

Lunch   One bowl of thick vegetable soup (see recipe on page 142) accompanied by a salad of green leafy vegetables, including watercress. (Watercress is a great calcium provider. Type Ds tend to suffer from calcium deficiencies, so give yourself a good portion!)

4 p.m.   Herbal tea (see above for varieties).

Dinner	Baked fennel and celeriac or a large jacket potato, served with the following braised vegetables: spinach, carrots, hispi cabbage, courgette and asparagus.

Day two

On rising	One glass of warm water with a thin slice of lemon.
Breakfast	Unleavened oat and buckwheat bread: mix ½ cup of organic oats with ½ cup of buckwheat flour or flakes. Blend with a little water until it achieves a thick and creamy consistency. Pour into a greased, shallow, ovenproof dish and bake in a warm oven for approximately 20 minutes until golden brown. When cooked, turn out of the dish onto a plate, spread with unsalted butter and top with slices of cucumber.
11 a.m.	Choose one of the following herbal teas: nettle or dandelion.
Lunch	One bowl of thick vegetable soup (see recipe on page 142) followed by a large raw salad of cucumber, carrot, fennel, lettuce (any variety) and watercress.

85

4 p.m.   Herbal tea (see above for varieties).

Dinner   One portion of steamed white fish –
choose from haddock, plaice, dover
sole, lemon sole, bream or sea bass.
Serve with baked fennel, baked
celeriac and the following steamed
leafy green vegetables: kale, asparagus,
Brussels sprouts and savoy cabbage.

Type E

Irritating foods
Alfalfa sprouts
Bamboo shoots
Banana
Beer
Cheese of all varieties but blue cheese in particular
Dates
Eggs
Mango
Nuts
Oranges
Raisins
Shellfish
Soy sauce
Strawberries
Tomato

Watermelon
Yeast products (all)

Soothing foods
Apples
Buckwheat
Butter
Cabbage
Carrots
Celery
Chives
Melon (with the exception of watermelon)
Nettles
Oats
Okra
Onions
Papaya
Parsley
Potato

Soothing drinks
Burdock root and leaf tea
Carrot and apple juice
Carrot, cabbage and parsley juice
Celery, cucumber and parsley juice
Liquorice root and leaf tea (you can purchase
liquorice root in most health food shops)
Yarrow, comfrey and peppermint tea

87

Mineral salt remedy
Silica
Kali Muir

Day one

On rising   One glass of warm water with a thin slice of lemon.

Breakfast   Unleavened oat bread: mix 1 cup of organic oats with a little water and a pinch of ginger or cinnamon to taste. Blend until you have a thick, creamy consistency. Pour into greased, shallow, ovenproof dish and bake in a warm oven until it is golden brown (approximately 20 minutes). When cooked, turn out of the dish onto a plate, spread with unsalted butter and top with slices of cucumber.

11 a.m.   Choose one of the following herbal teas: dandelion, nettle, parsley or celery.

Lunch   Large jacket potato topped with a knob of unsalted butter. Serve with a large green salad of lettuce (any variety), cucumber, celery, fresh parsley and carrot.

4 p.m.   Herbal tea (see above for varieties).

Dinner   Poached, grilled or steamed haddock
              served with a selection of the following
              braised vegetables: fennel, carrot,
              white cabbage, asparagus or
              courgettes. Cook with a large,
              chopped onion and some finely
              chopped garlic.

Day two

On rising   One glass of warm water with a thin
              slice of lemon.

Breakfast   Unleavened oat bread (see recipe on
              page 88 for cooking instructions).
              When cooked, spread with unsalted
              butter and top with cucumber.

11 a.m.   Herbal tea (see above for varieties).

Lunch   Leafy vegetable soup (see recipe on
              page 143).

4 p.m.   Herbal tea (see above for varieties).

Dinner   Grilled chicken breast (remove the
              skin first), served with a large raw salad   89

of lettuce (any variety), cucumber, carrot, watercress and grated celeriac. Accompany with a large jacket potato topped with a knob of unsalted butter.

Type F

Irritating foods

Alfalfa shoots
Aubergine
Bamboo shoots
Banana
Beer
Blue cheeses
Chocolate
Mayonnaise
Oranges
Peanut butter
Peanuts
Pumpkin seeds
Red wine
Shellfish
Soy sauce
Sunflower seeds
Sweet potato
Tomato
Vinegar
Watermelon

Soothing foods
Apples
Artichokes
Asparagus
Brussels sprouts
Butter
Cabbage
Carob
Carrots
Celery
Chichory
Chives
Courgettes
Cucumber
Grapefruit
Lemon
Lentils
Lime
Oats
Onions
Papaya
Paw Paw
Peach
Pineapple
Potato
Sorrel
Watercress

Soothing drinks

Cabbage, carrot, parsley and celery juice, *(juice
1/2 white cabbage, 3 carrots, 1/4 bunch parsley
and 2 sticks celery)*
Carrot and apple juice
Elderberry juice
Hot water with a slice of lemon

Mineral salt remedy

Ferr Phos
Kali Sulph

Day one

On rising   One glass of warm water with a thin
slice of lemon.

Breakfast   A selection (two pieces) of fresh ripe
juicy fruits: choose from apples (a
great cleanser), peaches, pears, kiwi
fruit, cherries or grapes. If you have
the time try stewing the fruit in a little
water, this softens and breaks down
the acid in the fruit so that your body
can more easily digest it. You must not
eat the following: banana, oranges or
watermelon.

11 a.m.   Apple tea (see recipe on page 157).

Lunch One large jacket potato served with a large raw salad of mixed leafy vegetables of your choice. If desired, dress the salad with lemon juice or pineapple juice.

4 p.m. Choose from one of the following herbal teas: dandelion, nettle or camomile.

Dinner Steamed, poached or braised white fish – choose from haddock, plaice, dover sole, lemon sole, bream or sea bass. Serve with a large helping of steamed or braised green vegetables, including onion and garlic. Add a knob of unsalted butter mixed with chives or parsley to the fish.

Follow with one large piece of juicy, ripe fruit (see list above for suggestions).

Day two

On rising One glass of warm water with a thin slice of lemon.

Breakfast Organic oat porridge. Mix 1 cup of organic oats with a small amount of water, bring to the boil and simmer until soft and creamy (approximately 15 minutes). When cooked, add half a grated apple.

11 a.m. Apple tea.

Lunch One bowl of thick vegetable soup (see recipe on page 142) followed by one large jacket potato topped with unsalted butter, finely chopped garlic and a handful of chopped fresh parsley.

4 p.m. Choose from one of the following herbal teas: dandelion, nettle or camomile.

Dinner One portion of sea bass – steamed, baked or grilled. Cook with finely chopped garlic and lemon juice to taste. When cooked, top with a knob of unsalted butter. Serve with steamed courgettes and savoy cabbage.

Note: avoidance of any kind of sexual stimulation is advisable during the treatment as sexual activity will over-stimulate the prostate gland.

Congratulations! You have now completed your two-day Face Type Plan. By now, your cravings should have disappeared like magic and, over the next couple of days, as you move on to the Core Diet, you should start to experience an extraordinary feeling of relaxation and wellbeing. You will already be feeling lighter and any bloating or water retention will be rapidly disappearing.

Now it's time to start the two-week Core Diet which *all* face types may follow. The same dos and don'ts as for the individual diets apply here, and you should keep including your soothing foods in the diet, while continuing to avoid your irritating foods. You'll see that the menus for each day are more varied and include a treat day for both weeks. Keep drinking your two litres of water each day and keep taking the appropriate mineral salt supplements as suggested.

Some people prefer to follow the Core Diet for just one week – particularly if holidays are planned or if you have a full diary – but I would always advise that you complete the entire two-week plan. The results will amaze you.

The Two-Week Core Diet

Week one

Day one

On rising One large glass of warm water with a thin slice of lemon.

Breakfast Organic oat porridge: mix 1 cup of organic oats with enough water to produce a thick and creamy consistency, then bring to the boil and simmer until soft (approximately 15 minutes). When cooked, add half a grated apple and three or four soaked dried prunes.

Alternative: Organic oat cakes. Spread with unsalted butter and top with cucumber and tomato. Four biscuits may be eaten at this meal.

11 a.m.   Choose one of the following herbal teas: camomile or peppermint.

Lunch   One large jacket potato topped with a knob of unsalted butter. Serve with a large raw salad of lettuce, cucumber, carrot, celery and watercress. Dress with 1 teaspoon of virgin first-pressed olive oil, mixed with crushed garlic and a squeeze of lemon juice.

4 p.m.   Herbal tea (see above for varieties).

Dinner   One portion of turkey breast – poached, grilled or stir-fried in a little water (do not use oil), with some crushed garlic and herbs to taste. Serve with the following green leafy vegetables: savoy cabbage, courgettes, broccoli and asparagus, topped with a little unsalted butter.

Day two

On rising   One large glass of warm water with a thin slice of lemon.

Breakfast   Unleavened oat and quinoea bread: mix ½ cup of organic oats with ½ cup of organic quinoea. Blend together with water until it has reached a thick and creamy consistency. Pour into a large, greased, shallow ovenproof dish. Bake in a warm oven until golden brown, approximately 20 minutes. When cooked, turn it out of the dish onto a plate and spread with unsalted butter.

Alternative: Four oatcakes *or* four amaranth biscuits. Top with unsalted butter and, if desired, some baby tomatoes and cucumber.

11 a.m.   Choose one of the following herbal teas: nettle, dandelion or lemon and lime.

Lunch   1 cup (dry measure) of buckwheat pasta topped with rich tomato and basil sauce (see recipe on page 148).

Serve with a large green leafy salad (no oil, no salt).

Alternative: A large jacket potato topped with a knob of unsalted butter and served with a green salad.

4 p.m.   Choose one of the following herbal teas: pear, camomile or peppermint.

Dinner   A portion of sea bass or dover sole, poached or grilled. Serve with the following steamed vegetables: kale, white cabbage, onions, carrots and fresh parsley. Add small knobs of butter to serve.

Day three

On rising   One large glass of warm water with a thin slice of lemon.

Breakfast   1 cup of unsweetened organic muesli. Add a little water rather than milk, to produce a creamy consistency.

11 a.m.   One green apple or one of the following herbal teas: lemon and lime or peppermint.

99

Lunch   A large jacket potato topped with garlic butter and sprinkled with mixed herbs, served with a large green leafy salad of lettuce (any variety), carrots, tomato and cucumber.

4 p.m.   Herbal tea (see above for varieties).

Dinner   One portion of chicken breast, braised or stir-fried in a little water (remember to remove the skin first). Serve with steamed courgettes, asparagus, white cabbage and chopped onion.

Day four

On rising   One large glass of warm water with a thin slice of lime.

Breakfast   1 cup of unsweetened granola. Soak in a little water overnight then add apple juice or pineapple juice to taste.

11 a.m.   Choose one of the following herbal teas: lemon and lime or peppermint.

Lunch   One bowl of thick vegetable soup (see recipe on page 142)

Alternative: Green salad with small baby potatoes topped with unsalted butter.

4 p.m.   Herbal tea (see above for varieties).

Dinner   A portion of poached or steamed sea bass with squeezed lemon juice. When cooked, add unsalted garlic butter. Serve with a large green leafy salad of radishes, cucumber, lettuce (any variety), carrot, endive, grated celeriac, chives and grated fennel. Dress with 1 tablespoon of olive oil with garlic, a squeeze of lemon juice and some mixed herbs.

Day five

On rising   One large glass of warm water with a thin slice of lemon.

Breakfast   Four organic oatcakes, spread with unsalted butter and topped with slices of cucumber.

11 a.m.   Choose one of the following herbal teas: peppermint or lemon and lime.

101

Lunch   Big chips (see recipe on page 152), served with a large green leafy salad.

4 p.m.   An apple.

Dinner   A portion of steamed or baked haddock, cooked with a squeeze of lemon and some crushed garlic. To serve, add a knob of unsalted butter and sprinkle with a pinch of cayenne pepper. Accompany with the following braised vegetables: savoy cabbage, carrots, garlic, peas and fennel. Slice the vegetables and place them in a pan with a little water. Bring to the boil and simmer until all the water has disappeared and the vegetables are soft and succulent.

Day six

On rising   One large glass of warm water with a thin slice of lemon.

Breakfast   Unleavened buckwheat bread: mix 1 cup of organic oats with 1 tbsp of buckwheat flour or flakes, adding a small amount of ginger or cinnamon to taste. Blend together with a little water until it has reached a thick, creamy consistency. Pour the mixture into a large, greased, shallow, ovenproof dish and bake in a warm oven for approximately 20 minutes until golden brown. When cooked, turn it out of the dish onto a plate, spread with unsalted butter and top with cucumber and tomato.

11 a.m.   Choose one of the following herbal teas: dandelion or nettle.

Lunch   A large jacket potato topped with a knob of unsalted butter and served with a large green salad of endive, lettuce (any variety), carrot, cucumber, mustard greens and watercress. Dress with 1 tbsp of olive oil with garlic, lemon juice and mixed herbs.

4 p.m.   Camomile tea.

Dinner   One portion of chicken breast, skin removed, grilled or fried in a little water (no oil) with garlic and herbs and a pinch of cayenne pepper, cumin, turmeric and cardamom (though omit the spices if suffering from stomach

103

ulcers). Serve with a chopped onion and the following green vegetables: collards, leeks, Brussels sprouts and savoy cabbage.

Day seven (treat day)

Breakfast   Toast made from soda or sourdough bread. Spread with unsalted butter and a teaspoon of sugar-free jam (*not* diabetic jam which contains saccharine), or alternatively try apple and pear spread (found in most health food shops) which is wonderfully sweet and gooey.

11 a.m.   Choose one of the following herbal teas: dandelion or nettle.

Lunch   One small portion of goats cheese (about 2.5 cm or 1 inch thick slice) and one large Granny Smith apple.

4 p.m.   Camomile tea.

Dinner   Chicken breast roasted with onions and garlic. Serve with a large baked potato, topped with unsalted butter, some savoy cabbage and asparagus.

Dessert	Tofuti ice cream with carob chocolate sauce (both available in good health food shops).

Week two

Day eight

On rising	One large glass of warm water with a thin slice of lime.
Breakfast	Organic oat porridge: mix 1 cup of organic oats with enough water to make a creamy consistency, bring to the boil and simmer until soft and succulent (approximately 15 minutes). When cooked, add 1 tbsp of unsweetened prune juice.
11 a.m.	Choose one of the following herbal teas: dandelion, nettle or camomile.
Lunch	A large green leafy salad of lettuce (any variety), cucumber, celery and carrot. Serve with steamed baby potatoes with parsley and unsalted butter.
4 p.m.	Water.

Dinner   A portion of haddock – poached, grilled or steamed. When cooked, add a knob of unsalted butter and some mixed herbs to taste. Serve with steamed asparagus, cabbage and carrots.

Day nine

On rising   One large glass of warm water with a thin slice of lime.

Breakfast   Millet porridge: mix 1 cup of millet with a little water, bring to the boil and simmer for 20 minutes until light and fluffy (it should look a little like rice). When cooked, add a knob of unsalted butter.

11 a.m.   Choose one of the following herbal teas: dandelion, nettle or lemon and lime.

Lunch   A large baked potato with unsalted butter served with a large raw salad of lettuce (any variety), white cabbage, endive and carrot.

4 p.m.   Herbal tea (see above for varieties) or water.

Dinner   A portion of dover sole – grilled,
             steamed or poached with lemon juice.
             When cooked top with unsalted garlic
             butter. Serve with the following
             braised vegetables: savoy cabbage,
             peas, carrots and squash. Put the sliced
             vegetables in a little water, bring to the
             boil and then simmer until all the
             water has evaporated.

Day ten

On rising One large glass of warm water with a
             thin slice of lemon.

Breakfast Quinoea porridge: mix 1 tbsp of
             quinoea with 1 cup of organic oats and
             a little water, until its produces a
             creamy consistency. Bring to the boil
             and simmer until soft (approximately
             15 minutes). When cooked, add 1 tbsp
             of grated apple or 1 tbsp of soaked
             dried figs and apricots in juice. (Pour
             boiling water over the dried figs and
             apricots. Rinse and repeat the
             procedure, but this time leave the
             dried fruit soaking in a sealed
             container overnight and use the
             resultant juice as an added sweetener.

107

Do make sure that you keep the fruit airtight overnight as bacteria loves uncovered fruit.)

11 a.m. Choose one of the following herbal teas: dandelion, nettle or camomile.

Lunch A large jacket potato with a knob of unsalted butter. One bowl of thick vegetable soup (see recipe on page 142).

4 p.m. Herbal tea (see above for varieties) or water.

Dinner A portion of skate – grilled, poached or steamed. When cooked, add a knob of unsalted butter with crushed garlic and chopped fresh parsley. Serve with the following vegetables: Swiss chard, courgettes, runner beans, cauliflower and broccoli.

Day eleven

On rising One large glass of warm water with a thin slice of lemon.

Breakfast Unleavened buckwheat and quinoea bread: mix 1 tbsp of millet flour, 1 tbsp of buckwheat flour or flakes, 1 tbsp of quinoea and 3 tbsp of organic oats. Add a little water and blend together until it has reached a thick and creamy consistency. Pour the mixture into large, shallow, greased ovenproof dish and bake in a warm oven for approximately 20 minutes until golden brown. When cooked, carefully turn out the bread onto a plate and spread with unsalted butter.

11 a.m.   Choose one of the following herbal teas: dandelion, nettle or camomile.

Lunch   Mashed potato made from one very large potato mixed with unsalted butter (no milk), served with steamed carrots, asparagus and courgette.

4 p.m.   Herbal tea (see above for varieties) or water.

Dinner   Braised chicken breast cooked with garlic and mixed herbs. Serve with the following roast vegetables: onion wedges, garlic, tomatoes, hispi cabbage and carrots.

Day twelve

On rising   One large glass of warm water with a thin slice of lemon.

Breakfast   Organic oat porridge: mix 1 cup of organic oats with enough water to make a creamy consistency, bring to the boil and simmer until soft (approximately 15 minutes). When cooked, add 1 tbsp of grated apple or apple juice.

11 a.m.   Choose one of the following herbal teas: dandelion, nettle or peppermint.

Lunch   Potato wedges (see recipe on page 153). Serve with tomato, lettuce, cucumber and carrot.

4 p.m.   Herbal tea (see above for varieties) or water.

Dinner   A portion of chicken breast, fried in a little water with some chopped garlic and herbs to taste. When the chicken is nearly cooked, add some onions and tomatoes and simmer until cooked through. Serve with steamed courgettes, fennel, green beans and carrots.

Day thirteen

On rising One large glass of warm water with a thin slice of lemon.

Breakfast Four organic oat cakes spread with unsalted butter and topped with slices of cucumber or unsweetened jam.

11 a.m. Choose one of the following herbal teas: dandelion, nettle or lemon and lime.

Lunch Cook 1 cup of brown rice, then toss in unsalted butter and serve with a green leafy salad of savoy cabbage, cabbage, grated carrot, chopped fresh chives and celery. Dress with 1 tbsp of olive oil with a squeeze of lemon juice and some crushed garlic.

4 p.m. Peppermint tea or water.

Dinner A portion of monkfish – grilled, steamed or poached. Add caraway or fresh parsley to taste. Serve with the

111

following steamed vegetables: savoy cabbage, spinach, courgette and carrots.

Day fourteen (treat day)

On rising   One large glass of warm water with a thin slice of lime.

Breakfast   1 cup of unsweetened muesli or Kashi (seven grain cereal available in health food shops). Top with 2 tbsp of plain goat's yoghurt and 1 tbsp of unsweetened prune juice.

11 a.m.   Choose one of the following herbal teas: dandelion, nettle or lemon and lime.

Lunch   A small jacket potato, served with a large green salad, a 2.5 cm/1 in thick slice of feta cheese and two large, plump olives.

4 p.m.   Herbal tea (see above for varieties) or water.

Dinner   Roasted chicken or turkey breast served with the following roasted vegetables: carrots, courgettes, onions and tomato.

Dessert   Baked Granny Smith apple stuffed with dried figs.

Now that you have completed the entire programme you will be feeling energetic and alert. You skin will be glowing, your hair will be shiny and glossy, your eyes bright and clear and you will have shed all those excess pounds. The changes this diet produces are really quite miraculous.

Core Diet Meal-Plan Variations

The following meal plans offer an alternative to those of the Core Diet in the preceding pages, but may also serve as your continuing maintenance plan. They also include some dessert options not listed in the original Core Diet. You should continue to take your 11 a.m. and 4 p.m. drinks.

Alternative breakfasts

☆ Mix ½ cup of organic oat meal and ½ cup of millet with enough water to make a creamy consistency. Bring to the boil and simmer until soft (approximately 15 minutes). When cooked, add fresh chunks of pineapple, grated apple, a squeeze of lemon juice and you might also like to scrape in some vanilla seeds for some extra flavour.

☆ 1 cup of granola with soya milk or goat's milk, topped with fresh raspberries or strawberries and a teaspoon of honey to sweeten.

☆ Unsweetened muesli topped with 3 4 tablespoons of stewed figs, apricots and almonds and the remaining juice from the fruits. (The night before, place six dried figs, six dried apricots and six whole almonds in a bowl and cover with hot water. Leave overnight, ensuring the bowl is covered to prevent bacteria forming. You can save any leftover fruit for another day's breakfast, but keep well covered and refrigerated.)

☆ Two thin slices of sourdough or soda bread. Toast until golden brown and spread with unsalted butter, topped with sliced, grilled cherry tomatoes.

☆ 1 cup of Kashir cereal (available in health food shops and some supermarkets). Add oat milk or soya milk and top with grated apple to sweeten.

☆ A portion of fresh, ripe, juicy fruit (choose from apples, papayas, pineapples, pears, or berries), served with 2 tablespoons of goat's yoghurt.

☆ Steamed pears (peeled and cored) served with 2 tablespoons of goat's yoghurt.

☆ Mix 1 cup of organic oats with 2 cups of water. Bring to the boil and simmer until soft and succulent (approximately 20 minutes). When cooked, add 1 tablespoon of stewed apples and 2 tablespoons of goat's yoghurt.

☆ Quinoea with fig and apricot sauce: the night before you want to eat this, cover six dried figs, six dried apricots, ½ tablespoon of flax seeds and ½ tablespoon of sesame seeds with warm water and leave to soak overnight, keeping well covered. The following morning, strain the fruit and then cover again with fresh warm water and blend until thick and creamy. Meanwhile, mix 1 cup of quinoea with 3 cups of water. Bring to the boil and simmer for approximately 15 minutes until the water has evaporated and the quinoea is soft and fluffy. Pour the fig and apricot sauce over the cooked quinoea, stir, then add a teaspoon of cream or goat's milk. Serve with a small glass of pineapple, apple or grapefruit juice to drink.

☆ The night before, soak the following in hot water: 2 tablespoons of almonds, 2 tablespoons of cashew nuts, 2 tablespoons of sesame seeds, adding 1 tablespoon of honey and 1 teaspoon of vanilla essence to the water. The following morning, rinse and drain the water, add 1 cup of apple juice and blend until creamy. Spoon the mixture over 1 cup of unsweetened granola – you may find there's enough for two days. Pour over a little soya milk or goat's milk if required.

☆ Unleavened corn bread (see recipe on page 142), topped with unsalted butter and 2 tablespoons of sugar-free baked beans.

☆ Couscous delight: mix 1 cup of couscous with ½–1 cup of water. Bring to the boil and simmer until light and fluffy. When cooked, add 1 teaspoon of honey and 1 teaspoon of cream and top with strawberries or raspberries.

☆ Pitted prunes topped with honeyed nuts and crème fraîche: wash six pitted prunes carefully then leave to marinate overnight in pineapple juice, keeping well covered. The next morning, sprinkle on some crushed almonds and cashew nuts and top with 1 tablespoon of crème fraîche, 1 teaspoon of honey and 1 teaspoon of lemon juice.

117

☆ Cantaloupe melon topped with freshly squeezed lemon juice and 1 tablespoon of crème fraîche.

Alternative lunches

☆ A large jacket potato with a knob of unsalted butter, stuffed with raw grated onion, carrot and fennel (or you may prefer to replace the fennel with celeriac).

☆ Thinly slice one large baking potato (washed, but unpeeled) and bake for approximately 25 minutes in a hot oven until golden brown, turning once during the cooking time. When cooked add garlic butter (made with fresh crushed garlic mixed with unsalted butter) and sprinkle with a pinch of turmeric. Serve your garlic chips topped with fresh parsley and a large green salad.

☆ One large jacket potato topped with garlic butter and served with a green leafy salad made from lettuce, cucumber, tomato, mung beans, alfalfa and radish, and dressed with 1 tablespoon of olive oil and lemon juice.

☆ A large bowl of leek soup (see recipe on page 144), followed by one jacket potato topped with butter.

☆ A bowl of thick green pea soup (see recipe on page 144), served with a slice of sourdough bread spread with unsalted butter.

☆ Thick vegetable soup (see recipe on page 142) topped with croutons made from toasted sourdough or soda bread. Serve with a salad of lettuce (any variety), endive, grated carrot and three cherry tomatoes, dressed with lemon or pineapple juice.

☆ Large baked potato, topped with garlic butter and 1 tablespoon of cottage cheese. Serve with a large salad of lettuce (any variety), carrot, celery, tomato, watercress and nasturtium leaves.

☆ Roasted vegetables: place two carrots (quartered lengthways), one large onion (peeled and quartered), two garlic cloves and one potato (cut into slices) onto a baking tray and brush with olive oil mixed with lemon juice and thyme. Place in a hot oven for approximately 30 minutes until golden and crispy. Serve with a salad of lettuce, watercress, celery, cucumber and tomato.

☆ Large bowl of carrot and coriander soup (see recipe on page 145), served with croutons

119

made from one slice of sourdough or soda bread, toasted and cut into cubes.

☆ Tofu veggie sarnies (see recipe on page 153).

☆ Barley and bay leaf soup (see recipe on page 146), served with a large green salad.

☆ Two thin slices of toasted sourdough or soda bread. Spread with unsalted butter and top with houmus (see recipe on page 147), romaine lettuce, cucumber and tomato. If you are a Type B, houmus should only be eaten in moderation – no more than one serving a week.

☆ A bowl of thick vegetable soup (see recipe on page 142) topped with croutons made with toasted sourdough bread. Serve with two thin slices of sourdough toast spread with unsalted butter.

☆ A bed of romaine lettuce topped with two slices of goat's cheese and a large stuffed tomato (see recipe on page 150).

Alternative dinners

☆ Roasted duck breast (though remember that duck is fattening if eaten too often, so stick to just one portion per week), served with steamed new potatoes topped with fresh mint. Accompany with braised carrots and courgettes.

☆ Braised chicken breast, glazed with a teaspoon of honey mixed with some fresh lemon juice and a pinch of Herbamare. Serve with stuffed cabbage leaves: parboil 1 cup of brown rice and a little seaweed (this is in place of salt), drain then spoon onto the cabbage leaves. Roll them up, place into a steamer and cook for approximately 5 minutes.

☆ Stir fried chicken: pour 1 cup of water into a large frying pan or wok and place on a high heat. Add two cloves of chopped garlic, some sprigs of thyme and three cardamom seeds and stir-fry quickly. Toss in one large chopped red onion and sauté until brown. Turn down the heat and add one chicken breast with the skin removed, cut into strips, to the frying pan. Fry gently until cooked (approximately 10 minutes) then remove from heat and serve with a large green salad.

121

☆ Steamed haddock, cooked with a little lemon juice and some finely sliced ginger. Add a knob of butter when cooked. Serve with braised carrots, broccoli and asparagus.

☆ Roasted chicken (with the skin removed) served with steamed, stuffed cabbage and steamed parsnips. When cooked, top with unsalted butter. Serve with a green salad made from watercress, lettuce (any variety), grated carrot and tomato.

☆ Grilled chicken breast (with the skin removed). Baste the chicken breast with lemon juice and chopped garlic, then add a knob of butter once cooked. Serve with 1 cup of brown rice and a large salad of lettuce (any variety), cucumber, tomato, grated carrot, grated celeriac, grated fennel, celery, endive and watercress.

☆ Fresh seabass, steamed or poached in a little soya milk. When cooked, add a knob of butter and a squeeze of lemon. Serve with braised broccoli, spinach, and sliced rings of onion.

☆ One sliced turkey breast (with the skin removed), served with a large salad of lettuce (any variety), spinach, celery, cucumber, radish and tomato. Dress with 1 tablespoon of olive oil and a squeeze of lemon or pineapple juice.

☆ Buckwheat noodles and vegetable goulash (see recipe on page 149). Serve with a green salad.

☆ Lentil loaf (see recipe on page 151), served with roasted savoy cabbage, asparagus and corn on the cob.

☆ Portion of grilled chicken breast (remove the skin), with braised courgettes, red onion, spring greens and white cabbage. Serve with tomato and basil chips. To make the chips, take one large baking potato, cut it into slices and bake in a hot oven for approximately 20 minutes until golden brown. Meanwhile, slice and grill three ripe tomatoes, then pour over a dressing made of 1 tablespoon of virgin olive oil, 1 tablespoon of lemon juice and 1 tablespoon of fresh basil. Spread the potato slices with the tomato topping and serve.

☆ Steamed sea bass served with steamed carrots, broccoli and courgettes and topped with butter and lemon juice.

☆ Roasted chicken breast (with the skin removed) served with cabbage creole (see recipe on page 151) and roasted carrots.

☆ One portion of steamed dover sole served with 1 cup of boiled brown rice and some steamed broccoli and courgettes.

Dessert options

☆ Fresh honeydew melon topped with fresh mint and a squeeze of lemon juice

☆ Core a large cooking apple, stuff with stewed dried figs and apricots (roughly three of each), and bake in a medium oven for approximately 30 minutes. When cooked, pour over the remaining juice from your stewed fruits. (To stew the fruit, place the dried figs and apricots in a bowl and cover with hot water. Leave overnight, ensuring the bowl is properly covered over to prevent bacteria forming.) Stewed dried fruit is also good as a dessert on its own.

☆ Wash and core two large pears, stuff with dried figs (stewed overnight in water, see previous recipe) and bake for approximately 30 minutes in a medium oven until soft. While the pears are baking, gently heat 1 tablespoon of honey, then pour over the cooked pears to serve.

☆ Tofuti ice cream with carob sauce (a chocolate alternative) and fresh fruit.

☆ Fig and prune pie (see recipe page 155).

☆ One oat cake topped with a slice of goat's cheese.

☆ Baked apple. Wash and core the apple and stuff with grated pine nuts. Bake the apple in a hot oven for approximately 30 minutes. When cooked, drizzle over 1 teaspoon of honey.

☆ Prune whip (see recipe on page 156).

☆ Honeydew melon topped with apple juice and plain yoghurt.

☆ Fresh cantaloupe melon topped with a mixture of 1 teaspoon of honey and 1 tablespoon of lemon juice.

Staying on track

In order to maintain your weight and new-found energy and vitality, I recommend that you substitute your own food type diet in place of your regular meals once a week. Many of my patients do this with marvellous results. You should also continue to leave out those irritating foods that apply to your type while incorporating your soothing foods and drinks.

PART THREE

Facial Analysis and Your Health

As you will have discovered by now, facial analysis and an understanding of the twelve mineral salts serve as important diagnostic tools and, if used correctly, they can help in correcting imbalances in the body and treating a range of deep-seated conditions. However, specific maladies will occur occasionally – such as headaches, colds or 'flu symptoms – but the good news is that facial analysis can help with this too. Over the following pages you will see how you can use facial analysis to treat these common health complaints, but first let's look more closely at another very useful method for diagnosing problems.

Tongue analysis

Tongue analysis, although not strictly belonging to the practice of facial analysis, nevertheless forms an important part of the work that I do with my patients and is one of the oldest diagnostic procedures.

The tongue is a large muscle enclosed in an array of nerves and fibres. It is the start of the

129

digest tract and so is an essential factor in determining the body's overall health.

Tongue analysis is very simple – it is simply a case of standing in front of a mirror, poking your tongue out and observing what you see carefully. A healthy tongue has a moist, pink surface, indicting the correct fluid balance within the body, and a pale red colouring owing to good blood circulation and a correct mixture of blood and fluids within the body. The clear fluids in the body serve as a blood thinner and so if there is a deficiency in these fluids the tongue will become a deeper red.

The following points will help you diagnose your own health problems and identify the tissue-salt remedy that will most help you.

☆ Taking antibiotics can cause the tongue to become coated with a grey film.

☆ An enlarged tongue can indicate underfunctioning of the thyroid gland. Treat this with the homeopathic remedy Fucus.

☆ A smooth pale tongue indicates nutritional deficiencies which can be corrected by a healthy diet and the tissue salt Calc Phos.

☆ A tongue falling to one side may well be a symptom of a stroke and you should consult a doctor. Taking Kali Phos may help to alleviate the symptom.

☆ A tremor of the tongue may indicate an overactive thyroid or the beginning of multiple sclerosis. Kali Phos should be taken.

☆ A very red colour at the tip of the tongue indicates excess acid within the body. You should increase the alkaline foods in your diet (see Appendix Two, page 161) and take the alkaline tissue salt Nat Phos.

☆ A pale red tongue with a slight swelling in the centre, a thin yellow coating and small red spots towards the back of the tongue may indicate faulty blood flow to the spleen. Taking Ferr Phos will help oxygenate the bloodstream.

☆ A pale grey tongue with teeth marks either side indicates an accumulation of dampness and an insufficient supply of blood to the spleen. Take four Ferr Phos salts three times a day.

☆ A red tongue with red sides and a dry thick white coating at the rear of the tongue indicates a lack of fluid in the stomach and poor blood flow to the kidneys. Correct this by increasing your daily intake of water and take Kali Sulph.

☆ A reddish tongue with pale edges and dark, pin-sized spots may indicate liver blood deficiency. Nat Sulph is the tissue salt necessary here.

131

☆ A thick grey-green coated tongue is a clear indication of chronic constipation. This can be rectified by administering a good dose of cleansing herbs (try Potter's cleansing herbs, available in health food shops) and some Nat Phos (and don't forget your daily two litres of water).

☆ A painful, pale tongue can indicate anaemia caused by a lack of iron in the diet or heavy smoking.

☆ Small ulcers or cankers in the mouth and on the tongue often indicate emotional stress, fatigue or a lowered immune system. Ensure you are getting plenty of Vitamin C in your diet (see Appendix One, page 158).

Headaches

Headaches are a strong indication of a lack of certain mineral salts. Here, I identify four common headache types, and describe how symptoms of the headache manifest themselves in the face. Look at the charts below in order to ascertain the most likely cause of your headache and the correct mineral salt you need to be taking in order to treat it effectively. Do note that any severe discomfort, pain or a rash should be acted upon immediately, and you may choose to seek medical advice.

Tension headache

Location of headache   A throbbing pain from the
neck upwards to the top
of the back of the head

Facial symptoms   Puffiness, swelling, a
silvery line underneath the
eyelashes, sponginess of
cheeks

Verdict   Tension headache, most
commonly caused by
stress and anxiety

Mineral salt remedy   Nat Muir

Fatigue headache

Location of headache   Pain or throbbing behind
the eyes

Facial symptoms   Dark rings under the eyes,
flushed face with red,
burning ears

Verdict   This headache is common
in students as it often
occurs after long periods
of concentration and study
in a stuffy room

Mineral salt remedy   Ferr Phos

Stimulus headache

Location   A vice-like feeling around
the top part of the head   133

Facial symptoms	Glossy, shiny nose tip, irritated skin, sunken eyes
Verdict	This headache is the result of severe stress levels especially when related to noise or light sensitivity
Mineral salt remedy	Silica

Nervous headache

Location	Shooting, darting, stabbing pains relieved by the application of heat, sparks before the eyes
Facial symptoms	Pinkish area around the nose
Verdict	Nervous headache, caused by prolonged periods of worry or excitement
Mineral salt remedy	Mag Phos

Menopause

I am often questioned on my views with regard to HRT. My reply is that I am strongly against any artificial drug used for ailments that can be successfully treated with herbal remedies when prescribed correctly.

What woman in her right mind would willingly ingest a pill consisting of a pregnant mare's urine (natural or synthetic)? Remember that the mare – who is kept in a constant state of gestation and in a space not big enough for a large cat – is getting rid of her toxic waste through urination. Remember too that menopause occurs naturally to *free* women from the hormones (progesterone and oestrogen) contained in the urine. I believe that with the correct diet, a few herbs, some mineral salts, vitamins and exercise, the latter years could be the most exciting, sexy and happy time of your life – *without* the use of artificial drugs. The diet tips and supplement suggestions below will help:

Soothing foods
Cabbage – white, red and savoy (cabbage contains
        large amounts of calcium, essential for women
        going through the menopause)
Brown rice
Tahini (a sesame spread, enriched with calcium)
Watercress
Dandelion leaves
Goat's cheese
Houmus
Potatoes
Fresh salmon and tuna
Plenty of fresh vegetables

135

Irritating foods

Sugars

Salt

Dairy products

Wheat

Sweet potato (too sugary)

Aubergine (too acidic)

Supplements

Black Cohosh – an excellent herbal remedy for
women going through the menopause

Mag Phos – should be taken to treat cramps

Uvi Ursi – a herb that should be taken to treat
general symptoms

Ferr Phos – will soothe vaginal inflammation

Vitamin and mineral supplementation

People often ask me what I think of vitamin and
mineral supplements. Cynics profess that all our
needs should be met in the food that we eat, which
is correct. However, how many of us can grow our
own organic food in a non-polluted environment
and pick it and eat it within the same hour?
Unfortunately, the truth is that our food is depleted
of its essential vitamins and minerals before it
reaches our table. It has been lurking in a
warehouse for days awaiting transportation. It is
often tightly packed in a cold storage container

travelling over land and sea for weeks, before
eventually landing at some retail outlet in the
middle of the high street, where the carbon
monoxide saturates our limp cabbage leaves and
lettuces.

In my opinion, therefore, supplements are not
only good for you but they are essential. I have
been in the health business for twenty years and I
have supplemented my diet with vitamins and
minerals for the same length of time. The following
are the most important:

Vitamin B is a lifesaver for stress
Vitamin E is essential for fertility
Vitamin C is an excellent bowel mover and
    immune system booster.

Of course, you should also try to maximize your
natural vitamin and mineral intake by buying fresh,
organic food. Appendix One (page 158) gives a list
of foods that are naturally rich in vitamins and
protein.

Constipation

Constipation is a common occurrence among the
people of the western world. However, it is
practically unknown in places such as Africa and
India where the legs at the end of the trunk are

137

used as nature intended. Walking is the first safeguard against constipation, so try ditching your car for a few weeks and feel the benefits of some light exercise.

I am amazed when my patients inform me that they empty their bowels every four to five days. Mother Nature in her wisdom will store this matter as fat just in case there is a famine. Where do they think that the waste from their pre-digested food is going? If the waste is not eliminated after meals, it hangs around and then is reabsorbed back into the bloodstream, fermented and toxic.

Constipation is caused by many factors but the most common are:

☆ Anxiety
☆ Lack of exercise (especially walking)
☆ Dehydration (you should try to drink 1–2 litres of water every day)
☆ Refusal to answer 'the call' promptly (how many of you are there who are 'far too busy' to go to the loo and then complain of constipation?)
☆ Piles (hard stools and dehydration, stomach and abdomen pain with an extended bloated feeling)

It has been reported that laughter is the best medicine; that being the case, try a good dose of comedy while sitting on the loo at the same time

every morning (preferably after breakfast). Read
the funniest material available.

Facial analysis for life

Facial Analysis has completely changed my life. And
it will change yours too. Over the many years I have
been practising, I have met thousands of people
from all walks of life and in all shapes and sizes who
have experienced the life-changing results of this
simple dietary plan. People who have spent years
dieting without success have found that this
unique and personalized technique has literally
transformed them. Time and time again I hear
them say just how incredible the transformation
has been.

You do not need to be an expert, all you need
is a mirror and the intention to look and see. By
following the plan that is right for *your type*, you
too will experience the most wonderful surge of
energy and vitality. As your body eliminates
unwanted toxins, watch and see as the most
amazing changes occur before your eyes. Your hair
will become glossy and strong, your skin will glow,
your eyes will take on a lustre as the new you
radiates from within and on the outside your body
will become sleek and firm.

It never ceases to surprise and delight me just
how beautiful my patients become. Cheek bones

appear that even they never realised were there, the jaw line becomes smooth and defined and lines around the forehead, mouth and eyes literally disappear.

With this physical transformation comes a great sense of security. You have harnessed a tool that will serve you throughout your life. You will feel in control of your health and immediately be able to see when you need to start cutting back on certain foods or replacing lost mineral salts. Simply by looking in the mirror you will be able to judge what it is that your body requires for optimum health.

With this sense of security there also comes an unimaginable new confidence. Your focus will change from pondering on what to have for dinner to celebrating a life free of toxins, cravings and over-indulgences. You will no longer crave that bar of chocolate or that plate of chips; food will no longer be a pre-occupation or an enemy, it simply will not be an issue. This transformation will motivate you to enjoy aspects of life that you never believed possible.

Whoever you are, it is never too late to set yourself on the path to vitality.

PART FOUR
The Recipes

Unleavened Corn Bread

1 tbsp soya flour
1 tbsp oatmeal flour
1 tbsp millet flour
1/2 cup golden cornflour
1 cup water

Blend together the dry ingredients. Then add the water and blend to a creamy consistency. Pour the mixture into a shallow ovenproof dish and bake in a warm oven (170°C/mark 3) for approximately 20 minutes or until the bread is firm to the touch and golden brown.

Thick Vegetable Soup

2 onions, chopped
3 cloves garlic, finely chopped
2 carrots, sliced
1/4 savoy cabbage, chopped
3 asparagus tips
pinch cayenne pepper
pinch turmeric
pinch cardamom

Gently fry the onions and garlic in a dry saucepan until they soften (be careful they don't burn), then add the vegetables and spices and continue to cook gently for 2–3 minutes. Cover the vegetables generously with water and bring to the boil, then allow to simmer until the vegetables have softened, approximatcly 20–30 minutcs. Lcavc to cool slightly and blend to a thick and creamy consistency. Reheat to serve.

Leafy Vegetable Soup

2 onions, chopped
3 cloves garlic, finely chopped
3 large leaves of kale, chopped
2 carrots, sliced
1/4 savoy cabbage, chopped
6 Brussels sprouts, cut into quarters
1/4 white cabbage, chopped
pinch cayenne pepper

Gently fry the onions and garlic in a dry saucepan until they soften (be careful they don't burn), then add the vegetables and continue to cook gently for 2–3 minutes. Cover the vegetables generously with water and bring to the boil, then allow to simmer until the vegetables have softened, approximately 20–30 minutes. Leave to cool slightly, then add the cayenne pepper and blend to a thick and creamy consistency. Reheat to serve.

Leek Soup

1 large red onion, chopped
2 cloves garlic, finely chopped
1 leek, sliced
¼ savoy cabbage, chopped
1 tsp Herbamare or approx. 900 ml/1½ pints
homemade stock

Gently fry the onion and garlic in a dry saucepan until they soften (be careful they don't burn), then add the vegetables and continue to cook gently for 2–3 minutes. Cover the vegetables generously with water and mix in the Herbamare, or use homemade stock if preferred. Bring to the boil and allow to simmer until the vegetables have softened, approximately 20 minutes. Serve immediately or leave to cool slightly and blend to a creamy consistency if preferred. Reheat to serve.

Thick Green Pea Soup

1 large onion, chopped
1 clove garlic, finely chopped
1 cup of green peas (preferably fresh,
    otherwise frozen)
¼ savoy cabbage, chopped
1 carrot, chopped

Gently fry the onion and garlic in a dry saucepan until they soften (be careful they don't burn), then add the vegetables and continue to cook gently for 2–3 minutes. Cover the vegetables generously with water, bring to the boil and allow to simmer for approximately 20 minutes until the vegetables have softened. Leave to cool slightly, then blend, reheat and serve.

Carrot and Coriander Soup

1 large onion, chopped
2 cloves garlic, finely chopped
5 carrots, chopped
1 stick of celery
1 tbsp parsley
1 tbsp fresh coriander

Gently fry the onion and garlic in a dry saucepan until they soften (be careful they don't burn). Add the vegetables and herbs and continue to cook gently for 2–3 minutes. Cover generously with water, bring to the boil and allow to simmer for 20–30 minutes until soft and flavourful. Leave to cool slightly, then blend, reheat and serve.

Barley and Bay Leaf Soup

1 large onion, chopped
2 cloves garlic, finely chopped
1 carrot, chopped
2 bay leaves
pinch sage
pinch oregano
pinch Herbamare
¼ cup soaked whole barley kernels
    (not pearl barley)

Gently fry the onion and garlic in a dry saucepan until they soften (be careful they don't burn). Add the carrot and herbs and continue to cook gently for 2–3 minutes. Cover generously with water, mix in the Herbamare and add the barley. Bring to the boil and allow to simmer for approximately 20 minutes. Leave to cool slightly, remove the bay leaves then blend until creamy. Reheat before serving.

Houmus

1 head garlic, finely chopped
1 onion, chopped
1 cup chickpeas, canned or dried
½ cup tahini
1 tbsp sesame oil
2 tbsp lemon juice
pinch of salt

If you're using dried chickpeas, soak them overnight, then drain off the water and rinse. Place in a pan, cover with water, bring to the boil and cook until soft (approximately 1 hour, or 10 minutes if you have a pressure cooker). Drain, reserving a little of the cooking water. You can omit this preparation if you are using canned chickpeas as they are already cooked.

Pour the chickpeas into a blender along with the rest of the ingredients. Blend until it has reached a creamy, golden consistency, adding a little water to loosen the mixture if necessary.

Rich Tomato and Basil Sauce

1 tsp pressed organic virgin olive oil
1 onion, chopped
1 clove garlic, finely chopped
2 large tomatoes, chopped
1 tbsp fresh sweet basil, chopped
1/2 tbsp fresh thyme, chopped
pinch cayenne pepper
pinch cardamom

Heat the olive oil in a large pan and gently fry the onion and garlic until soft. Add the chopped tomatoes, sweet basil, thyme and spices and heat gently for a minute or so. Cover with water, bring to the boil and simmer gently for 20–30 minutes until rich and flavourful.

Buckwheat Noodles and Vegetable Goulash

1 cup 100% buckwheat noodles
1 pinch Herbamare
4 florets broccoli
4 florets cauliflower
1 large onion, chopped
5 asparagus stems, chopped

FOR THE DRESSING:
2 tbsp lime juice
1 tbsp honey
1 tbsp basil
1 tbsp dill
2 tbsp virgin olive oil
1 tbsp parsley, chopped

Mix together all the ingredients for the dressing, cover and put to one side. Ideally the flavours should be left to infuse together for at least 2 hours before you prepare the noodles.

Place the noodles in a large pan of boiling water along with a pinch of Herbamare. Cook uncovered for approximately 15 minutes then drain. Meanwhile, steam the broccoli, cauliflower, onion and asparagus, then place in the centre of the noodles. Toss in the dressing and serve.

Stuffed Tomato

1 large ripe beef tomato
½ small onion, finely chopped
¼ carrot, chopped
½ cup peas
pinch Herbamare
1 tsp Tamari

Cut the top off the tomato, scoop out the insides using a teaspoon and discard. Gently fry the onion, carrot and peas in a dry frying pan until slightly softened, then add the Herbamare and Tamari. Transfer to a blender and blend roughly together until smooth. Scoop the mixture into the tomato and bake in a medium oven for approximately 30 minutes or until the tomato is cooked through.

Cabbage Creole

1 small savoy cabbage, cut into quarters
1 onion, chopped
1 tbsp parsley, chopped
1 tsp basil
1 tsp rosemary
1 tsp cardamom
2 ripe tomatoes, chopped

Mix together the cabbage, onion and herbs and place in a steamer. Top with chopped tomatoes and steam until tender. Serve.

Lentil Loaf

1 large onion, finely chopped
2 cloves garlic, finely chopped
1 carrot, chopped
1 large potato, chopped
1 tomato
1 cup red lentils, soaked overnight
2 tbsp pinhead oatmeal
1 tbsp parsley

Gently fry the onion and garlic in a dry saucepan until soft (be careful they don't burn). Add the remainder of the ingredients and cover with water. Bring to the boil, then simmer for approximately 20

151

minutes until the vegetables and lentils are soft. Drain, reserving a little of the excess water, then place in a blender and blend until creamy, adding water as necessary. Place the mixture in a loaf tin and bake in a medium oven until golden brown, approximately 15 minutes. Leave to cool slightly then turn out of the tin and slice to serve.

Big Chips

1 large baking potato, sliced
unsalted butter
2 cloves garlic, finely chopped
mixed herbs to taste, chopped

Preheat the oven to a medium temperature. Leaving the skin on, slice the baking potato into thick chips approximately 2.5 cm/1 in wide. Place on a baking sheet and bake on the top rack of the oven for approximately 20 minutes, turning the chips over halfway through the cooking time. Remove from the oven when both sides are golden brown.

Mix together the butter with the garlic and herbs and spread over the hot chips until melted.

Potato Wedges

1 large baking potato
unsalted butter
handful fresh chives, finely chopped

Preheat the oven to a medium temperature.
Leaving the skin on, slice the baking potato into
quarters and then slice each quarter again. Place on
a baking sheet and bake in the oven for
approximately 30 minutes, turning the wedges
once or twice during the cooking time. Remove
from the oven when golden brown. Top with
knobs of butter and sprinkle over the fresh chives.

Tofu Veggie Sarnies

2 thin slices of sourdough or soda bread
125g/4 oz firm tofu
½ small onion, chopped
½ cucumber, chopped
1 tbsp parsley, chopped
1 tbsp carrots, chopped
1 tbsp virgin olive oil
handful mung bean sprouts
½ tsp Tamari

Lightly toast the sourdough or soda bread. Mash
the tofu in a bowl and add the rest of the

153

ingredients with the exception of the mung beans and the Tamari. Blend together until creamy then spread thickly on the toast. Serve topped with the mung bean sprouts and Tamari.

Stuffed Cabbage

2 large leaves of savoy cabbage
handful of green leaves
1 onion, finely sliced
1 clove garlic, finely chopped
½ cup couscous

Mix together the beansm onion, garlic and couscous and spoon half the mixture onto the middle of one cabbage leaf and theremainder onto the second. Carefully fold up the laves and place into a steamer. Steam for 5–7 minutes and serve.

Fig and Prune Pie

8 dried pitted prunes, soaked overnight
8 dried figs, soaked overnight
3 tbsp water
1 tbsp honey
1/4 cup sesame seeds
1 tsp cinnamon

FOR THE PIE CRUST:
1 cup oats
1/2 cup water
1 tsp vanilla extract

To make the pie crust, mix together the oats, water and vanilla extract then line a shallow dish with the mixture, pressing it up into the sides. Bake in a warm oven for approximately 20 minutes until golden brown. When cooked, remove from the oven and leave to cool.

For the filling, blend together the fruit, water, honey, sesame seeds and cinnamon in a blender. Pour into the pie crust and serve immediately.

Prune Whip

8 dried pitted prunes
6 dried apricots
2 tbsp flax seed
6 almonds
6 cashew nuts
1 cup water
1 tbsp goat's yoghurt

Soak the fruit and nuts overnight in a little water.
Blend together the fruit and nuts with the water
until smooth and creamy. Top with the yoghurt
and serve.

Celery and Parsley Tea

3 sticks celery
1 bunch fresh parsley
approx. 300 ml/½ pint water

Wash the celery and parsley and place them in a
pan. Cover with the water and bring to the boil.
Allow to simmer for 10–15 minutes, then strain and
drink.

Apple Tea

3 Granny Smith apples
approx. 300 ml/½ pint water

Wash and peel the apples and place the peel in a
pan. Cover with the water and bring to the boil.
Allow to simmer for about 20–30 minutes, until the
apple flavour is absorbed. Strain and drink.

Stock

Never throw away vegetable peelings (including
pea pods and onion peelings). Wash them well,
place in a pot and cover with water. Bring to the
boil and simmer for 30 minutes until full of flavour,
then strain with a sieve. This will make an excellent
base for soups. Stock will keep in a refrigerator for
1–2 days, or you can reduce it down and freeze in
ice cube trays for later use.

Vitamin- and Protein-Rich Foods

Foods rich in vitamin A (betacarotene)
Apricots
Broccoli
Carrot
Chinese cabbage
Parsley
Peaches
Peas
Pumpkin
Radish leaves
Spinach
Squash
Swiss chard
Tomatoes
Watercress

Foods rich in vitamin B
Apricots
Asparagus
Beans (dried)
Broccoli
Brussels sprouts
Grains
Lentils
Olives
Pears (dried)
Pumpkin
Soya beans

Foods rich in vitamin C
Apricots
Chicory
Cranberries
Grapefruit
Kohlrabi
Lemon
Lime
Mustard greens
Olives
Orange
Parsley
Soya beans
Tomatoes
Watercress

High-protein foods (non-animal)
Almonds
Beans
Butternut squash
Lentils
Oatmeal
Pine nuts
Pistachio nuts
Walnuts

An Alkaline- and Acid-Balanced Diet

An important discovery that I have made through my development of the Facial Analysis Diet is that optimum health can be possible if the correct pH balance is maintained in the diet. The pH level is a measure of how much acid or alkaline is in a substance. I learned that if the body's cells are not bathed in a fluid which has the correct pH acid-alkaline balance, the cells will die prematurely.

Saliva should have a neutral pH, the enzymes of the stomach's gastric juices should have an acid pH, while urine should be alkaline. If any of these pHs are thrown out of balance due to a poor diet, the digestive enzymes become inactive and food cannot be properly digested.

To accomplish the correct pH, balance, I became familiar with acid- and alkaline-forming foods (see list below). The results were amazing.

Within months I was running up mountains and dancing until dawn – and I was on the trail of a very exciting mode of recovery without the aid of orthodox drugs and their harmful side effects.

Foods are separated into two groups: acid foods and alkaline foods. The phrases 'acid forming' or 'alkaline forming' indicate the effect that foods have within the body during the digestive process.

The acid/alkaline content is determined by the elements contained in the food. If the elements in the food are dominated by iodine, phosphorus sulphate and chloride then the food is classified as 'acid forming'. However, if the elements contain substantial amounts of calcium, potassium, magnesium and sodium the food will be categorized as 'alkaline forming'. All foods contain some or both elements but one or the other will be dominant.

Acid-forming foods are not always so obvious. For example, lemon, lime and grapefruit are acidic in the mouth but change to alkaline in the stomach through the digestive process and when the 'ash' is analyzed the verdict is alkaline. The mild organic acids in these foods are cleansing to the body and are beneficial during a detox programme because of their antioxidant effect. However if the fruit is picked before it has ripened the effect will be

extremely acidic both in the mouth and in the

stomach. The orange, on the other hand, is acid and should not be eaten by asthma sufferers.

Each of the six plans work to limit the amount of acid-forming foods in the diet. Excess acid can cause heartburn, reflux and, if combined with a stressful lifestyle, stomach ulcers. It is unlikely for a person to suffer from excess alkaline. But it is important to maintain a balance.

Alkaline-Forming Foods

Dairy
Buttermilk
Milk
Yoghurt

Vegetables
Asparagus
Cabbage
Carrots
Celery
Cucumber
Dandelion leaves
Endive
Horseradish
Kelp
Kohlrabi
Leeks
Okra

Onion
Parsley
Parsnips
Radish
Sorrel
Spinach
Turnips
Watercress

Fruits
Apples (especially baked)
Apricots (fresh)
Berries
Cantaloupe
Cherries
Figs
Grapefruit
Guava
Lemon
Lime
Melon (all except watermelon)
Olives
Papaya
Peaches
Pears
Pineapple

Acid-Forming Foods

Meat
All meats
All poultry
All shellfish

Fruits
Canned fruits
Cranberries
Dried fruits
Glazed fruits
Plums
Prunes

Other foods
All alcohol
All flour
Barley
Coconut
Coffee
Corn
Macaroni
Marmalade
Mayonnaise
Oats
Pasta
Pastry
Pies

Roasted nuts (all, especially peanuts)
Soda water
Vinegar
Wholegrains